1000

EXTREME
&
EXTRAORDINARY
DINOSAUR
FACTS

This edition published by Parragon Books Ltd in 2015 and distributed by

Parragon Inc.
440 Park Avenue South, 13th Floor
New York, NY 10016
www.parragon.com

Written by Gill Davies
Designed, produced, and packaged by Cloud King Ltd

ISBN 978-1-4723-7932-0

Printed in China

Discovery KIDS™

1000

EXTREME & EXTRAORDINARY DINOSAUR FACTS

PaRragon

Bath · New York · Cologne · Melbourne · Delhi
Hong Kong · Shenzhen · Singapore · Amsterdam

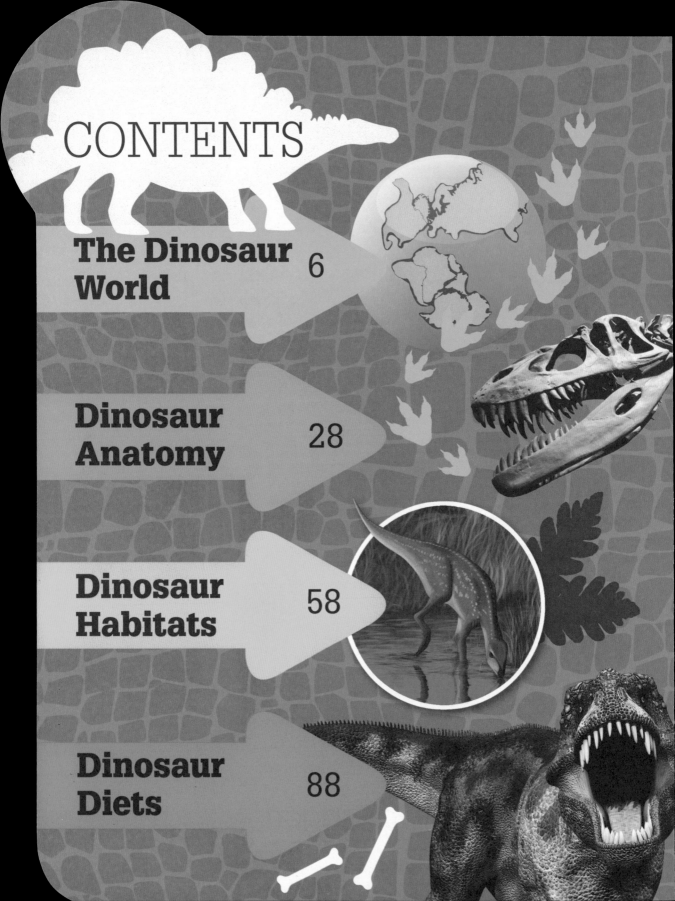

CONTENTS

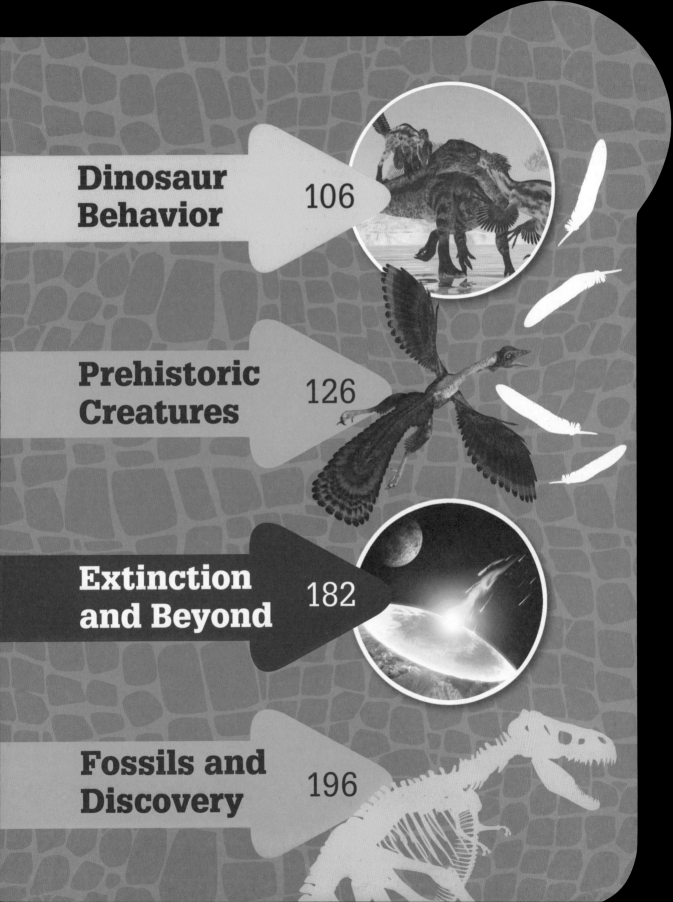

THE DINOSAUR WORLD

CHAPTER 1

Dinosaurs are among the **MOST AMAZING** creatures ever.

They roamed Earth for more than 160 million years—that's **820 times longer** than modern humans have existed. #0001

FACTS ABOUT

8 BEING A DINOSAUR

THE WORD DINOSAUR MEANS "TERRIBLE LIZARD,"

but although dinosaurs were reptiles, they were **NOT** actually lizards! #0002

Dinosaurs lived on Earth during the **Mesozoic Era,** 252 to 66 million years ago.

#0003

DINOSAURS may have been the most **SUCCESSFUL** creatures ever to live on

EARTH.

#0004

SOME DINOSAURS were as small as a chicken; **others were BIGGER than a truck.**

#0005

The flying **pterosaurs** and swimming **plesiosaurs** of the Mesozoic Era were **NOT dinosaurs.**

#0006

Some dinosaurs ate only **plants**; others hunted or scavenged for **meat.**

#0007

DINOSAURS WERE LAND ANIMALS, ALTHOUGH SOME **EVOLVED INTO BIRDS.**

#0008

Unlike today's lizards and crocodiles, whose legs stick out from the sides of their bodies, a dinosaur's pillarlike legs were set **DIRECTLY BENEATH IT.**

#0009

9

8 FACTS ABOUT PLANET DINOSAUR

When dinosaurs first lived on Earth, there was just one **GIGANTIC supercontinent. Called PANGAEA,** it was the only land mass within a vast ocean. #0010

The climate of **Pangaea** was **HOT** and **DRY.** #0011

Pangaea formed an **INCREDIBLE 300 TO 270 MILLION YEARS AGO.** #0012

The name **Pangaea** comes from the Greek words "*pan*" and "*gaia*", which mean "Mother Earth." #0013

Pangaea covered almost **ONE-THIRD** of Earth's surface, just as the continents do today.

#0014

The one **VAST** global ocean surrounding Pangaea was **named Panthalassa.**

#0015

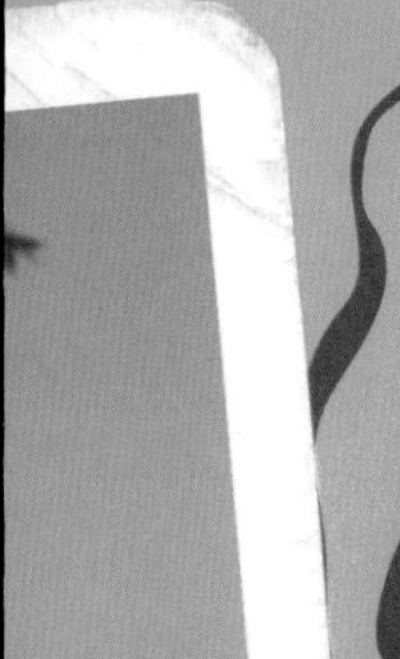

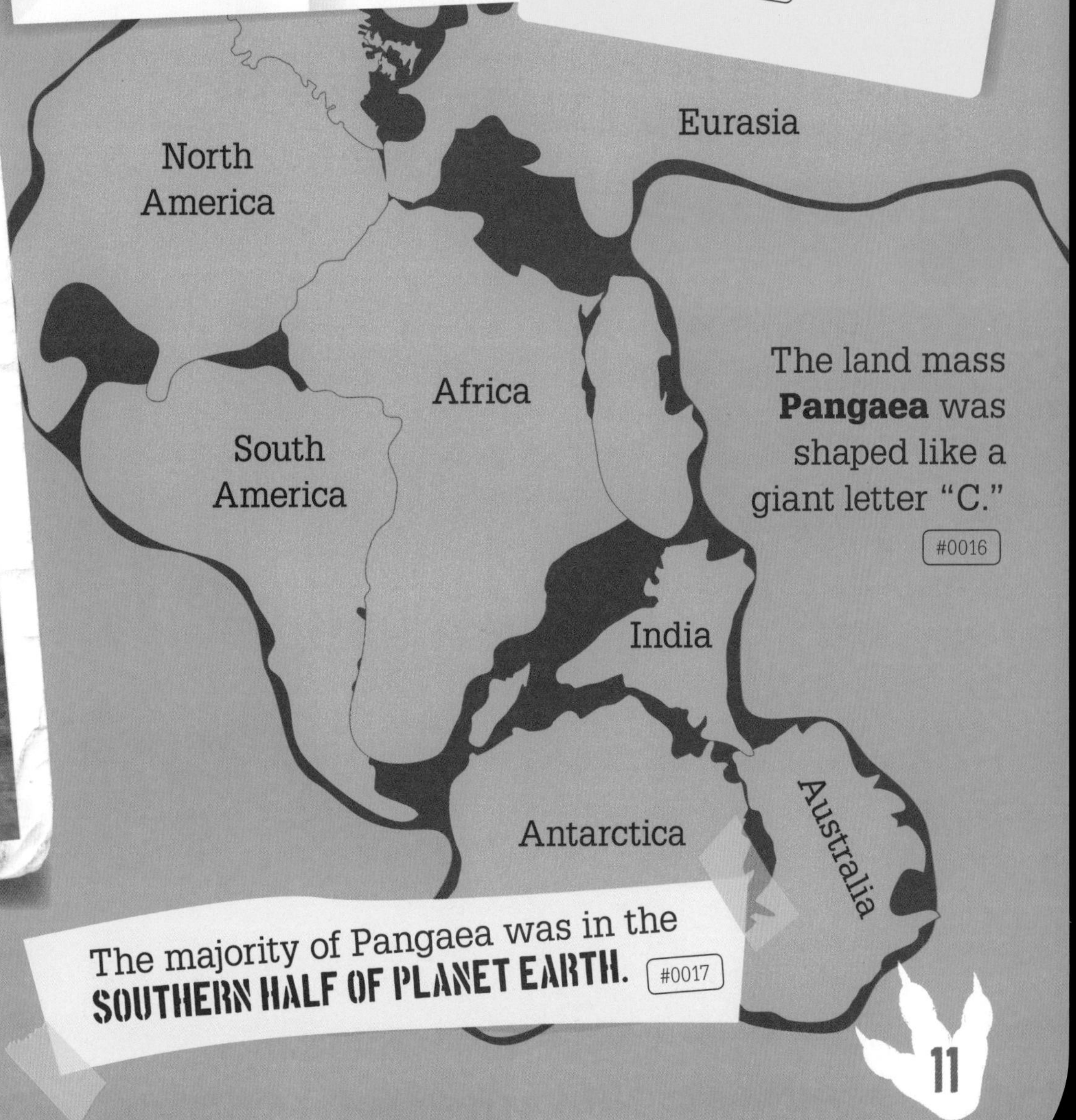

North America

Eurasia

Africa

South America

The land mass **Pangaea** was shaped like a giant letter "C."

#0016

India

Antarctica

Australia

The majority of Pangaea was in the **SOUTHERN HALF OF PLANET EARTH.** #0017

11

7 FACTS ABOUT THE CHANGING WORLD

Laurasia
North America
Eurasia
Gondwana
South America
Africa
India
Tethys Ocean
Antarctica
Australia

About **175 MILLION YEARS AGO,** Pangaea began to break up into **two new SUPERCONTINENTS**— Laurasia and Gondwana.

#0018

As Pangaea broke up, vast rifts between the continents created

NEW oceans and seas.

#0019

The new continents brought huge climate changes.

#0020

For a while, **LAURASIA** and **GONDWANA** were linked by land.

#0021

DINOSAURS CROSSED

over the land between the two supercontinents. #0022

As the **climates** across the continents **changed,** the **variety** of dinosaurs, plants, and other animals **increased.** #0023

By the end of the Mesozoic Era, **Earth's land masses** had separated to become today's seven continents.

#0024

13

11 FACTS ABOUT THE
DINOSAUR TIMELINE
#0025

The Mesozoic Era, the age of the dinosaurs, is divided into three periods: the Triassic, Jurassic, and Cretaceous.

#0025

MASS EXTINCTIONS

are caused by vast ice sheets, volcanic eruptions, earthquakes, or asteriods slamming into Earth.

#0026

TRIASSIC
252 to 201 million years ago

Reptiles, such as rhynchosaurs, **DOMINATED** the land during the Triassic. #0028

The first **DINOSAURS,** mammals, and crocodilians appeared in the Triassic.

#0027

JURASSIC
201 to 145 million years ago

CRETACEOUS
145 to 66 million years ago

#0034

At the end of the Cretaceous, there was a **MASS EXTINCTION**, and most of the dinosaurs died out.

#0035

About **16 PERCENT** of ocean species died out at the end of the Cretaceous.

Ammonites flourished in the **Jurassic** seas.

#0032

During the Jurassic, **dinosaurs EXPANDED** into many new habitats.

#0030

ARCHAEOPTERYX, the first ever bird, appeared.

#0031

Jurassic plants included ferns, cycads, rushes and conifers, which all provided **FOOD** for the dinosaurs.

#0029

There were more **kinds** of dinosaur in the **Cretaceous** than ever before, including the horned **CERATOPSIANS.**

#0033

9 FACTS ABOUT THE TRIASSIC PERIOD

The very **FIRST** dinosaurs appeared in the middle of the **Triassic.** #0036

The Triassic lasted

51 MILLION YEARS,

from 252 to 201 million years ago. #0037

For some of the

TRIASSIC,

it was so hot that vast, baking deserts stretched across the land. #0038

The **TRIASSIC OCEANS** were filled with creatures such as **ammonites** and large **sea reptiles** called ichthyosaurs. #0039

Triassic **polar regions** were covered with **lush forests** rather than snow and ice.
#0040

There were no birds, but the **Triassic skies** were filled with **flying reptiles** called pterosaurs.
#0041

The first mammals appeared toward the end of the **TRIASSIC.**
#0042

The **TRIASSIC CLIMATE** was generally **warmer** than today.
#0043

Throughout the entire Triassic, there were no flowering plants and
#0044 **NO GRASS.**

12 FACTS ABOUT THE JURASSIC PERIOD

The Jurassic lasted for **56 million years.** #0045

The Jurassic began **201 million years ago** and ended **145 million years ago.** #0046

THE JURASSIC SEAS WERE FULL of ichthyosaurs, horseshoe crabs, plesiosaurs, giant crocodilelike creatures, sharks, rays, and ammonites. #0048

The vast Jurassic forests were full of tall tree ferns, ginkgoes, giant horsetails, mosses, pines, and many other conifer trees. #0047

A few early shrewlike mammals crept around in the Jurassic foliage. #0049

HUGE sauropods, such as DIPLODOCUS ...

The sturdy Jurassic stegosaurs, such as *Stegosaurus*, had **BODY PARTS** that they could use in their defense, such as tail spikes. #0050

18

Jurassic pterosaurs, such as **Pterodactylus**, had a wingspan of up to 3 feet. #0051

During the Jurassic, both **HUGE PLANT-EATING** species and smaller meat-eating ones spread across the continents. #0052

The first **BIRDS** flew in the busy Jurassic skies. #0053

The **JURASSIC STEGOSAURS** were dinosaurs with double rows of **HARD PLATES** along their backs. #0054

... and **BRACHIOSAURUS** lived in the Jurassic. #0055

Allosaurus was a mean, **DANGEROUS** Jurassic dinosaur that fed on stegosaurs and sauropods. #0056

7 FACTS ABOUT THE CRETACEOUS PERIOD

The **Cretaceous** saw the abundance of many animal groups, including **insects, mammals,** and **birds**. New dinosaur groups included pachycephalosaurs, ceratopsians, and hadrosaurs. #0057

Flowering plants probably first appeared in the **early Cretaceous** and eventually dominated the landscape. #0058

The oldest fossil of a flowering plant is **ARCHAEFRUCTUS LIAONINGENSIS,** which grew in the Cretaceous and is **125 million years old!** #0059

The Cretaceous lasted from **145 to 66 MILLION YEARS ago** and was the longest and last period of the **Mesozoic Era.**

#0060

Cycads, ferns and conifers

grew throughout the Cretaceous. New trees with broad leaves, such as oak, beech, and walnut, began to appear as the climate became more varied.

#0061

During the **Cretaceous,** some pterosaurs, such as **Quetzalcoatlus,** had wingspans of up to 30 feet.

#0062

Although the Cretaceous ended with a **mass extinction** of dinosaurs, many flowering plants, mammals, and insects lived on.

#0063

21

6 DINOSAUR NEIGHBORS

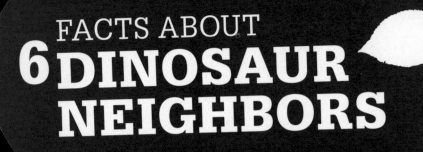

MINIBEASTS

such as flies, mosquitoes, wasps, and bees shared the dinosaur world. #0064

Insects became **TRAPPED IN AMBER,** a sticky resin from trees, and their fossils were **FOUND** millions of years later! #0065

Cretaceous leafhoppers jumped from leaf to leaf, sucking sap from trees.

#0066

Modern bees and wasps first appeared in the Cretaceous. They collected nectar from the new flowering plants. #0067

Tiny antlike beetles called *Kachinus*, just 0.02 inches long, scuttled around in the Cretaceous undergrowth.

#0068

INSECTS SCAVENGED DINOSAUR CORPSES.

#0069

Some of them, such as cockroaches and possibly early types of dung beetle, may have cleared up their droppings.

23

11 FACTS ABOUT
DINOSAUR RELATIVES

Dinosaurs were reptiles, but not all reptiles were dinosaurs.
#0070

Scutosaurus was a large Triassic reptile that roamed the floodplains in large herds, probably making **LOUD BELLOWS.**
#0072

Scutosaurus had a **horny head** protected by **spikes** and **plates.** #0071

Smooth-skinned amphibians evolved into scaly reptiles more than **300 MILLION YEARS AGO.**
#0073

Before dinosaurs took over the land, semiaquatic creatures called crocodilians were among the most **FEARSOME REPTILES.**

They dominated their water's-edge habitat for more than **200 MILLION YEARS.** #0074

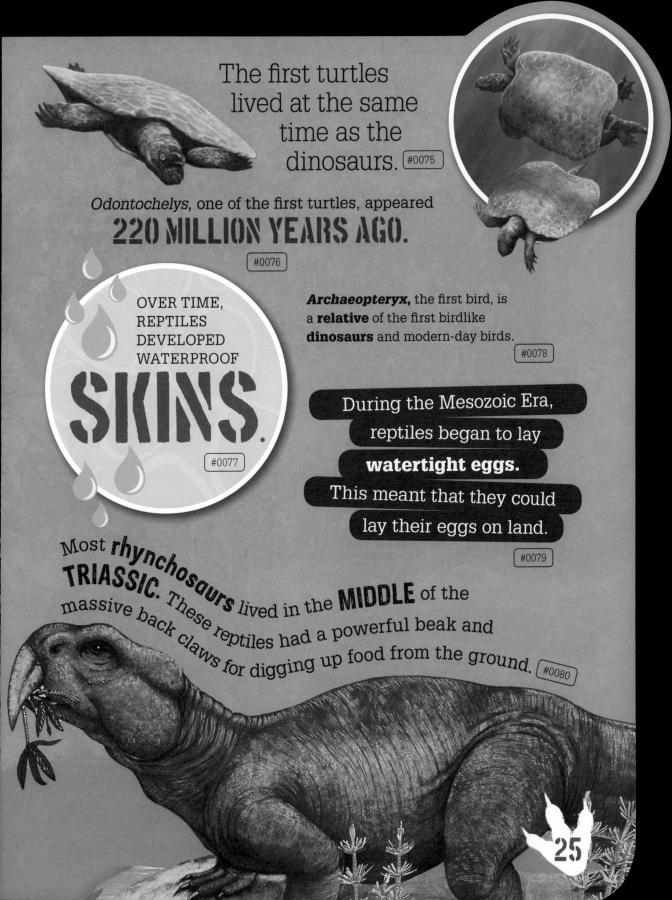

The first turtles lived at the same time as the dinosaurs. #0075

Odontochelys, one of the first turtles, appeared **220 MILLION YEARS AGO.**
#0076

OVER TIME, REPTILES DEVELOPED WATERPROOF **SKINS.**
#0077

Archaeopteryx, the first bird, is a **relative** of the first birdlike **dinosaurs** and modern-day birds.
#0078

During the Mesozoic Era, reptiles began to lay **watertight eggs.** This meant that they could lay their eggs on land.
#0079

Most **rhynchosaurs** lived in the **MIDDLE** of the **TRIASSIC.** These reptiles had a powerful beak and massive back claws for digging up food from the ground. #0080

DINOSAUR WORLD
FACT FILE

The fierce **meat-eater** T. REX was one of the **biggest** Cretaceous predators.

#0081

Grasslike plants have been found in fossilized **DINOSAUR POO** dating back **65 MILLION YEARS** —10 million years earlier than they were thought to have grown!

#0082

DURING THE CRETACEOUS **EXTINCTION,** DEBRIS FROM AN ASTEROID IMPACT DARKENED THE SKIES AND STARVED THE EARTH OF SUNLIGHT.

#0083

PALEONTOLOGISTS TELL US THAT MANY **DINOSAURS** WERE COVERED IN

#0084

FEATHERS.

Big land dinosaurs **existed on Earth** for **160 MILLION YEARS,** whereas modern **HUMANS** have been around for only **200,000 years.**

#0085

Dinosaurs lived in **ANTARCTICA** as the Poles were ice-free back then. In 1986, their fossils were found there.

#0086

Today's crickets have **ancient relatives** that lived at the same time as dinosaurs in the **JURASSIC FORESTS.**

#0087

SO FAR, FOSSILS OF AROUND

1,000

DIFFERENT TYPES OF DINOSAURS HAVE BEEN DISCOVERED.

#0088

Some **dinosaurs** were similar to modern-day **ostriches,** and perhaps **RAN JUST AS FAST.**

#0089

Not all early mammals were tiny. **REPENOMAMUS** grew to nearly **3 feet long** and

ATE DINOSAURS.

#0090

BEFORE MUCH WAS KNOWN ABOUT DINOSAURS, THEIR **REMAINS** WERE THOUGHT TO BE THE BONES OF **GIANTS** OR **OGRES.**

#0091

SHARKS

have swum in our oceans for over #0092 **400 MILLION years.**

DINOSAURS

are members of a large group of extinct animals that scientists call

DINOSAURIA.

#0093

In 1824, the first land dinosaur was named *MEGALOSAURUS* ...

... nearly **150 years** after its fossil bones were first found!

#0094

DINOSAUR
ANATOMY

Dinosaurs were TOUGH!

Their bodies could recover from injuries and infections that would kill most animals today. #0095

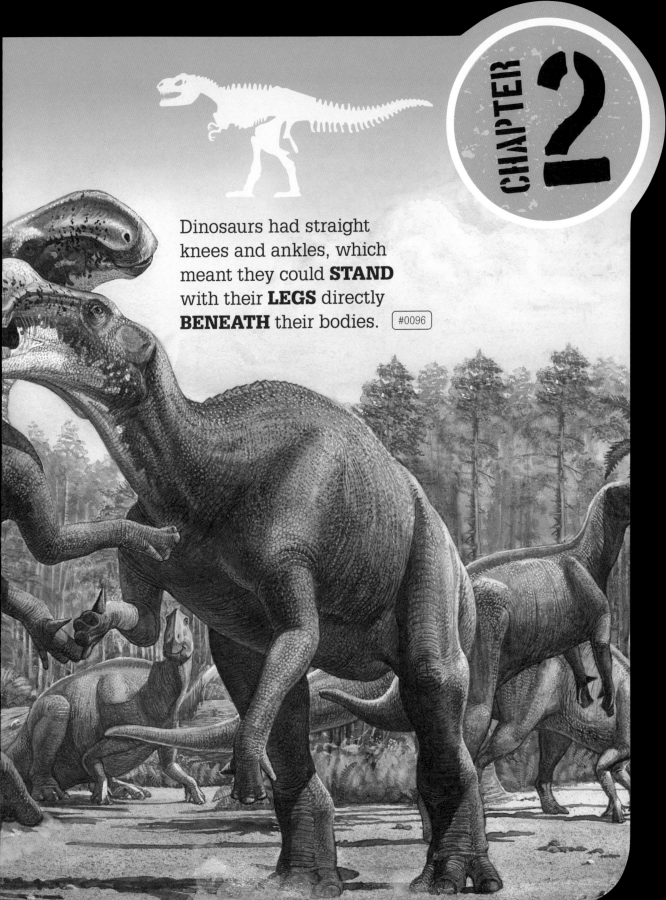

Dinosaurs had straight knees and ankles, which meant they could **STAND** with their **LEGS** directly **BENEATH** their bodies. #0096

12 FACTS ABOUT SIZE

Sauropod dinosaurs, such as Brachiosaurus, were **SO TALL** that they make today's giraffes look **really short!**

#0098

The **largest animal ever** is NOT a dinosaur but the **blue whale.**

#0099

Camarasaurus was an incredible 59 feet long.   #0100

Ornitholestes 6.5 feet long   #0101

Dilophosaurus 20 feet long   #0102

Torosaurus 25 feet long   #0103

Giganotosaurus 41 feet long   #0104

A baby **Tyrannosaurus rex** was only 10 feet long, but a growth spurt when it was about 14 years old meant it quickly reached full size.

#0105

Tyrannosaurus rex was fully grown by the time it was 19 years old.

#0106

It is likely that dinosaurs were warm-blooded rather than cold-blooded, since it takes a lot of internal heat to grow quickly.

#0107

Argentinosaurus ...

... was longer than three buses lined up end to end.

#0108

Dinosaurs were covered in very tough, scaly hides and sometimes had soft

FEATHERS, TOO. #0109

The fossil skin impressions left on **Carnotaurus'** fossil bones reveal many disklike scales. #0110

For a long time, the color and texture of dinosaur skin were completely unknown to the scientists who studied them. #0111

Carnotaurus' scales were like a mosaic with large pebblelike **BUMPS.** #0112

Scientists believe that *Sinosauropteryx* was covered in **orange feathers** and ...

... had a STRIPED TAIL.

#0113

The dinosaurs that evolved into birds had skin that was much thinner and lighter than nonbird dinosaurs.

#0114

 Skin pigments in the fossils of two prehistoric sea reptiles—a

196-MILLION-YEAR-OLD

ichthyosaur and an

86-MILLION-YEAR-OLD

mosasaur—were almost black. This suggested to scientists that dinosaur skin may have been black, too.

#0115

Amazingly, fossilized ***Anchiornis* feathers** have been found containing traces of **COLOR** pigments, showing that they were black, white, and gray.

#0116

33

9 FACTS ABOUT BODY ARMOR

Some **DINOSAURS** had large plates of **BONY ARMOR, SPIKES AND CLUBBED TAILS.**

#0117

The first armored dinosaurs had **BONY SCALES (SCUTES),** just like crocodiles.

#0118

Pentaceratops had **five horns:** a nose horn, two cheek horns, and a horn above each eye.

#0119

MIGHTY 2.2 ton ankylosaur *Euoplocephalus* had spikes and a CLUBBED TAIL. #0120

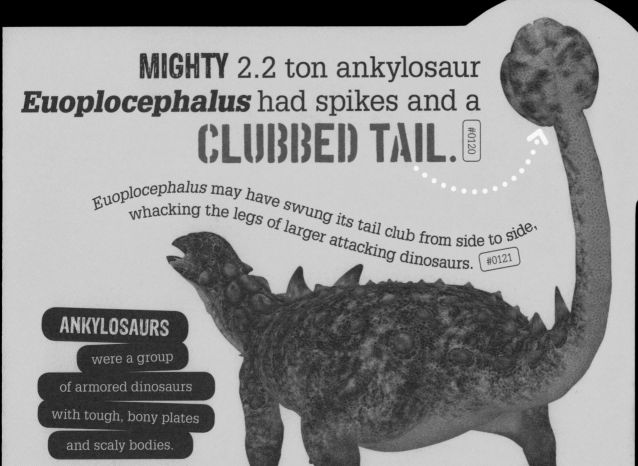

Euoplocephalus may have swung its tail club from side to side, whacking the legs of larger attacking dinosaurs. #0121

ANKYLOSAURS were a group of armored dinosaurs with tough, bony plates and scaly bodies. #0122

Euoplocephalus had **BONY EYELIDS**, which protected its eyes. #0123

Each of *Stegosaurus'* plates were around **30 to 31.5** inches tall. #0124

Stegosaurus' plates were covered in keratin, the same substance of which human hair is made. #0125

35

7 FACTS ABOUT DINOSAUR CLAWS

Therizinosaurus had GIGANTIC FRONT CLAWS 3 FEET LONG.

#0126

Therizinosaurus used its **claws** when feeding by **grabbing** leafy branches, **stripping** bark from trees, and maybe even **tearing open** termite mounds.

#0127

Claws may have been displayed to scare off enemies or attract mates.

#0128

Some meat-eating dinosaurs, such as *Deinonychus*, had **DEADLY CLAWS**, which they used to slash at their victims.

#0129

The name *Deinonychus* means **"TERRIBLE CLAW."**

#00130

Deinonychus had a deadly, retractable claw on each foot.

#0131

Some dinosaurs used their claws to kill their prey; others used them to hold down their prey, keeping their victim in a deadly grip before finishing it off with a **FATAL BITE.**

#0132

11 FACTS ABOUT DINOSAUR MOVEMENT

Dinosaurs walked on tiptoe rather than on flat feet. #0133

Tyrannosaurus rex could possibly run at **19 miles per hour**— that's as fast as a modern-day polar bear can run. #0134

Dinosaurs probably used their **long, stiff tails** for balance as they walked and ran. #0135

Scientists study **FOSSILIZED** dinosaur footprints to work out how **FAST** dinosaurs could **MOVE.** #0136

Compsognathus was a tiny dinosaur that may have been able to reach speeds of more than 37 miles per hour. #0137

FOSSILIZED DINOSAUR TRACKS

prove that **dinosaurs walked** with their tails held above the ground. #0138

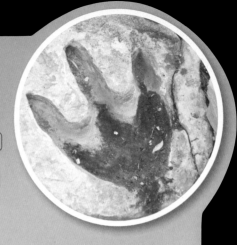

Dinosaurs walked with their toes pointing **inward.** #0139

Dreadnoughtus, a **MASSIVE**, recently discovered dinosaur, left **FOOTPRINTS** the size of washing machines. #0140

LARGE QUADRUPEDAL

(four-legged) dinosaurs, such as *Alamosaurus*, moved slowly at **about 5 miles per hour**. #0141

Some of the BIRDLIKE DINOSAURS may have flapped their feathered arms to help them **move faster.** #0142

Giant sauropods had long, flexible necks so they could feed over a wide area by swinging their necks, and standing still. #0143

Many of the **earliest dinosaurs** were bipeds.

#0144

Bipedal dinosaurs walked on **TWO FEET,** not four.

#0145

Theropods were a group of bipedal dinosaurs that included **TOP PREDATORS.**

#0146

Like all raptors, *Utahraptor* was a **SWIFT-RUNNING** biped.

#0147

BIPEDAL DINOSAURS

could run farther than most reptiles today.

#0148

While *Spinosaurus* usually **WALKED ON TWO LEGS,** it may have occasionally crouched and rested on all four.

#0149

OTHER BIPEDAL DINOSAURS INCLUDE: **Albertosaurus, Allosaurus, Baryonyx, Eoraptor, Gallimimus, Megalosaurus, Oviraptor,** and **Troodon.**

#0150

Bipeds included both **MEAT-EATERS** and **PLANT-EATERS,** but almost all quadrupedal (four-legged) dinosaurs were plant-eaters.

#0151

Some bipedal dinosaur species had arms that, **OVER MILLIONS OF YEARS,** evolved into wings.

#0153

Dinosaurs with **HEAVY** heads, horns, and neck frills, such as Triceratops, could not have walked on two legs without toppling over.

#0152

Some meat-eaters that walked on two legs used their forelimbs to grab prey, but not ***Tyrannosaurus rex***—its arms were much too short!

#0154

9 FACTS ABOUT DINOSAUR BRAINS

Scientists study **bird** and **crocodile** brains as a way of better understanding dinosaur brains.
#0155

Dinosaur relative **Archaeopteryx** had enlarged brain regions for control over sight. #0156

Many Triassic **PLANT-EATERS** had very small **brains** but a good sense of smell. #0157

Cretaceous plant-eaters like *Edmontosaurus* had slightly **bigger brains** than Jurassic plant-eaters, but their brains were still smaller than those of the dinosaurs that ate them! #0158

In proportion to its size, **ARCHAEOPTERYX's** brain was similar to the brains of modern-day birds.
#0159

TROODON

had a **large brain** in relation to its small body, making it probably one of the **smartest dinosaurs.**

#0161

To hunt prey at speed, dinosaurs needed bigger brains. #0160

Velociraptor had a **BIG BRAIN** for its size. It also had excellent eyesight and hearing. #0162

Tyrannosaurus rex had a **BIGGER BRAIN** than any plant-eater.

#0163

43

TEETH

Duckbilled dinosaurs, called hadrosaurs, had horny, toothless beaks, but up to

1,000 **cheek teeth**
in the sides of their jaws.

#0164

DINOSAUR-EATING
prehistoric crocodiles, found in the Sahara Desert in Africa, included **FEROCIOUS *KAPROSUCHUS.***

It had three sets of **DAGGER-SHAPED** fangs for slicing up meat.

#0165

44

Turkey-sized **Heterodontosaurus,** whose name means "different-tooth lizard," had three kinds of teeth plus a beak. #0166

Heterodontosaurus had **sharp** incisors for

CUTTING,

chisel-like teeth for **grinding,** and tusklike teeth for **DEFENDING ITSELF!** #0167

All dinosaurs **replaced lost teeth** by growing new ones. #0168

TYRANNOSAURUS REX'S
teeth were as **BIG AS BANANAS,** but a lot harder. They were strong enough to **crush bone.** #0169

Meat-eating dinosaurs such as **TYRANNOSAURUS REX** used their huge, sharp teeth to make a kill, usually by biting the neck of their prey. #0170

FACTS ABOUT
11 FEATHERED DINOSAURS

Feathers helped to insulate dinosaurs and keep them warm.
#0171

In the 1990s, fossil discoveries showed that many **DINOSAURS HAD FEATHERS.**
#0172

One set of fossilized dinosaur feathers contains **beta keratin,** a protein found in modern-day bird feathers.
#0173

Feathers may have first appeared

220 MILLION YEARS AGO
IN THE TRIASSIC PERIOD.
#0174

In the late 1800s, biologist **Thomas Henry Huxley** was the first person to show that birds were descendants of some of the feathered dinosaurs.
#0175

Feathers were most common among small theropod dinosaurs, such as *Caudipteryx.*
#0176

FEATHERS;

Others show quill knobs—bumps
where the feathers were attached. #0177

The first fossil of a feathered plant-eating dinosaur was
discovered in 2014. This showed that **BOTH MEAT-EATING
AND PLANT-EATING DINOSAURS** may have had feathers.
#0178

Feathered
dinosaurs existed
for around
**100 MILLION
YEARS.** #0179

**NOT ALL
FEATHERED
DINOSAURS
EVOLVED
INTO BIRDS.**
#0180

About 30 species of

feathered dinosaurs

have been identified.

#0181

47

FACTS ABOUT
9 BEAKS, BILLS, AND CRESTS

Erlikosaurus was a therapod dinosaur with a **HARD SNOUT** that was covered with keratin, just like a bird's beak.

#0182

Erlikosaurus' tough snout may have stopped its skull from being shaken when it battered hard food.

#0183

A hadrosaur dinosaur's duckbill was more than half as long as its skull.

#0184

Scientists think that hadrosaur duckbills evolved to replace teeth.

#0185

Ceratopsian dinosaurs, such as *Triceratops*, had small beaks.

#0186

Daspletosaurus' **HUGE HEAD** was probably used to knock its prey unconscious.

#0187

48

A dinosaur's beak was like a multi-tool penknife because it functioned as so many tools in one. It was used for: 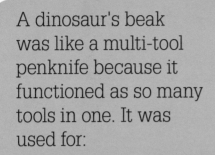 **feeding, protection, cleaning, and preening.** #0188

As well as their **tough duckbills,** some hadrosaurs had a hollow crest on the top of their heads, which made

LOUD HORN BLASTS.

#0189

Crests may have helped **HADROSAURS** such as **CORYTHOSAURUS** to recognize each other.

#0190

49

FACTS ABOUT
DINOSAUR SIGHT

7

Dinosaurs probably had **BETTER VISION** than most other prehistoric reptiles.

#0191

Plant-eater *Camarasaurus* had **eyes on the sides of its head,** giving it a wide field of vision with which to spot danger.

#0192

Predatory dinosaur *Troodon*

HAD LARGE EYES,

which were probably useful for hunting at **dusk and dawn.**

#0193

50

Deinonychus may have been able to see in the dark.

#0194

Like most of the meat-eating therapods, *Aucasaurus* had **forward-facing** eyes, which helped it to judge the distance to its prey. #0195

BECAUSE SOME DINOSAURS HAD BRIGHT FEATHERS AND CRESTS, SCIENTISTS THINK IT IS POSSIBLE THAT THEY COULD SEE IN COLOR. #0196

Leaellynasaura probably had good night vision since it lived close to the South Pole, where winter days are short and nights are long. #0197

8 FACTS ABOUT
HEARING AND SMELL

MEAT-EATERS didn't only track down live animals. Their **good sense of smell** helped them to find dead animals, too.

#0198

All **dinosaurs had ears** with eardrums and inner ears, just as humans do.

#0199

Large plant-eating dinosaurs could hear low-pitched sounds, and small plant-eaters high-pitched sounds.

#0200

Plant-eaters needed a

GOOD SENSE OF SMELL

to sniff out the best plants to eat.

#0201

Meat-eating dinosaurs used their powerful sense of smell to detect low-flying pterosaurs. #0202

PLANT-EATERS

may have used their sense of smell to find a mate. #0203

The 69-foot-long sauropod **JOBARIA** had very large nasal openings and was likely to have had a sharp sense of smell. #0204

A dinosaur's **inner ear** was used as much for **BALANCE** as it was for hearing. #0205

53

8 FACTS ABOUT DINOSAUR POO

Just like bones, **dinosaur poo** became fossilized and survived for **MILLIONS OF YEARS.** #0206

Fossil **poos** are called **coprolites.** #0207

Some **DINOSAUR POO** can tell us which food types a **dinosaur may have eaten.** #0208

54

Dinosaur poo helped fertilize the soil, so that plants could grow, keeping the forests lush and green.

#0209

Researchers now think that **cockroaches** ATE DINOSAUR POO. #0210

If sold at auction,

DINOSAUR POO

attracts huge amounts of money

—even **thousands of dollars.** #0211

Dinosaur coprolites range in size from a fraction of an inch to more than **2 feet—** as long as a child's arm! #0212

A scientist who studies dinosaur poo is called a paleoscatologist.

#0213

LITTLE AND LARGE
FACT FILE

ARGENTINOSAURUS

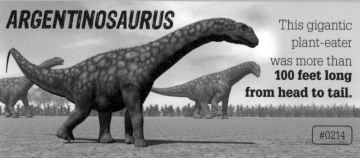

This gigantic plant-eater was more than **100 feet long** from head to tail.

#0214

A SINGLE **ARGENTINOSAURUS** SPINAL COLUMN VERTEBRA WAS OVER **4 FEET THICK!**

#0215

Argentinosaurus is the **longest** dinosaur ever found and, weighing up to **110 TONS**, it was the **HEAVIEST LAND ANIMAL EVER.**

#0216

A 66-TON, 85-FOOT *Dreadnoughtus* specimen discovered in Argentina was a youngster and still had **MORE GROWING TO DO.**

#0217

DREADNOUGHTUS
was **TEN TIMES HEAVIER** than *Tyrannosaurus rex.*

X 10

#0218

SPINOSAURUS
may be the **biggest meat-eating dinosaur,** possibly even **larger** than *Tyrannosaurus rex* and *Giganotosaurus.*

#0219

Giraffatitan was **85 feet long** and was the **largest** *animal to walk the Earth.*

#0220

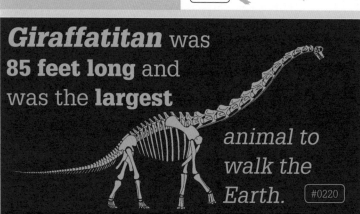

LEAELLYNASAURA'S TAIL WAS THREE TIMES LONGER THAN ITS BODY. #0221

Brachiosaurus weighed up to **88 TONS ...** ... that's as much as 17 **AFRICAN ELEPHANTS.** #0222

AT LESS THAN **3 FEET TALL,** the little plant-eater ***Lesothosaurus*** was the size of a **BIG TURKEY** and weighed only 9 to 15 pounds. #0223

Brachiosaurus was about **50 feet tall,** but the massive *Sauroposeidon* was possibly **even taller at 60 feet.** #0224

The **longest** DINOSAUR HORNS, at more than **3 FEET LONG,** were probably those belonging to ***COAHUILACERATOPS.*** #0225

THE SMALLEST **DINOSAUR EGGS** SO FAR FOUND WERE LAID BY *MUSSAURUS* AND WERE ONLY **AN INCH LONG.** #0226

THE BIGGEST DINOSAUR EGGS were probably laid by ***Hypselosaurus*** or ***Gargantuavis***— each egg was **AS BIG AS A BASKETBALL.** #0227

DINOSAUR HABITATS

Dinosaurs are SUPERSURVIVORS!

For over almost **165 MILLION** years, dinosaurs and other prehistoric creatures adapted to climate changes and lived **EVERYWHERE ...**

... from deserts to forests and from swamps to mountains.

#0228

6 FACTS ABOUT DESERT DINOSAURS

Many Triassic dinosaurs lived in dry, harsh landscapes alongside **lizards** and **early mammals.**

#0229

LARGE bodies helped desert dinosaurs keep cool—just like today's **ELEPHANTS!**

#0230

Fossils of **PROTOCERATOPS** and **VELOCIRAPTOR in mortal combat** were preserved by a fierce desert sandstorm 80 million years ago.

#0231

PLATEOSAURUS lived in dry areas with scrubby plant growth. It may have had to travel long distances to find food.

#0232

60

GIGANTORAPTOR

had splayed toes to
help it walk on soft
sand without sinking. #0233

When the blazing
SUN became too hot,
ANKYLOSAURUS may
have dug out a nice
cool pit in which to rest.
#0234

8 ROAMING THE PLAINS

For most of the **Mesozoic Era,** plant-eating dinosaurs ate the leaves of low-growing plants, shrubs, and trees on **wide-open areas of land** known as **plains.** #0235

Hundreds of thousands of plant-eating dinosaurs such as *LAMBEOSAURUS* roamed the plains in herds.

#0236

Each year, herds of *CAMARASAURUS* migrated more than **186 miles** across the plains to the mountains, looking for food.

#0237

With nowhere to hide, **CERATOPSIAN DINOSAURS** such as *Triceratops* had to keep a constant watch for predatory theropods.

#0238

Some horn-faced ceratopsians, such as **PROTOCERATOPS** and **ZUNICERATOPS**, roamed across the vast, dusty, windswept plains. #0239

Plants such as ferns grew on the plains and provided food for *RHINOREX* and *LATIRHINUS,* the duckbill hadrosaurs that grazed there. #0240

Scientists know that *TYRANNOSAURUS REX* hunted dinosaurs that lived on the plains because the digested remains of a *Triceratops* have been found in its **FOSSILIZED POO**. #0241

HUGE
SAUROPODS, SUCH AS **ARGENTINOSAURUS,** LIVED ON THE PLAINS. #0242

9 FACTS ABOUT
LIFE IN THE MOUNTAINS

On **steep mountain slopes,** rain washed away the soil, making it almost impossible for fossils to form.
#0243

During the **MESOZOIC ERA, new mountains** formed as **Earth's crust pushed up** over a **long** period of time. #0244

A **200-MILLION-YEAR-OLD** *Diplodocus*-like dinosaur named *Glacialisaurus* was found on Mount Kirkpatrick, Antarctica.
#0245

Scientists do **not know** if dinosaurs lived in mountainous areas because **few fossils** have been found there.
#0246

Armored dinosaurs such as **EDMONTONIA** may have lived high in the mountains, but when they died, their bones were **washed down** to lower areas.
#0247

During the late Jurassic period 140 million years ago, the **SEVIER MOUNTAINS** formed in what is now North America. #0248

In 2008, fossil bones of a dinosaur called *SUSTUT* were found in British Columbia, Canada. *Sustut* was the first dinosaur to be discovered in the **Canadian mountains** and may even be a **new species!** #0249

New mountain ranges shaped the evolution of dinosaurs, cutting off dinosaurs from the rest of the land, so that they evolved into new species. #0250

Dinosaur fossils found in the remote Antarctic mountains could belong to a new species, possibly related to *Heterodontosaurus*. #0251

FACTS ABOUT

6

FOREST DINOSAURS

When dinosaurs roamed **ANTARCTICA** 160 million years ago, it was warmer and had **forests!**

#0252

Forest-dwelling **ARCHAEOPTERYX** flew above the trees and lakes of what is now **WESTERN EUROPE,** and stalked small prey that lived along the riverbanks.

#0253

Prehistoric conifers had **tough needles** that helped them survive cool climates and protected them from most of the hungry, tree-eating dinosaurs, such as **DRYOSAURUS.**

#0254

BRACHIOSAURUS

used its 26-foot-long neck to feed on leaves found on the highest treetops. #0255

In Asian forests, **MAMENCHISAURUS** dinosaurs traveled in herds, their long necks parallel to the ground, probing between the forest trees to find foliage, horsetail, and ferns.

#0256

Brachiosaurus munched its way through **immense conifer forests,** enjoying even the tough-needled monkey puzzles and cypresses.

#0257

7 FACTS ABOUT RIVERSIDE DWELLING

GALLIMIMUS may have eaten insects, grubs, and plants by sieving river mud with the comblike plates in its mouth.
#0258

Dinosaurs didn't live in rivers; they prowled around the edges. Some, such as **SPINOSAURUS,** may have been very good at catching fish.
#0259

GALLIMIMUS ran at almost **43 miles per hour** along the riverbank mud.
#0260

We know that packs of **COELOPHYSIS** lived by rivers because **fossil footprints** have been found in what is now the United States.
#0261

Rivers flowed down from the uplands to bring life-giving water into desert areas for dinosaurs such as **PLATEOSAURUS** and **LILIENSTERNUS.**

#0262

River **MOSASAURS** were **dangerous, meat-eating reptiles** that fed on small crocodiles, turtles, and other fish.

#0263

River-dwelling **MOSASAURS** grew up to **20 FEET** in length.

#0264

10 FACTS ABOUT WETLAND DINOSAURS

Swampy, wetland areas were home to many dinosaurs, including **POLACANTHUS** and the small **HYPSILOPHODON.**

#0265

In the early Cretaceous, low-lying plains became **flooded** with water and sediments from hilly areas to create **wetlands.**

#0266

WETLANDS ARE **SOGGY, BOGGY** LANDS THAT COVERED MUCH OF THE AREA THAT IS NOW EUROPE DURING THE CRETACEOUS.

#0267

At more than **33 FEET LONG,** wetland dinosaur *IGUANODON* was bigger than an **elephant!**

#0268

Wetland sauropods, including **BRACHIOSAURUS,** fed on the horsetails and ferns that grew at the edges of the swamps.

#0269

Spiny **POLACANTHUS** was a squat, four-legged, plant-eating dinosaur that grazed on low-growing, wetland plants.

#0270

HYPSILOPHODON was a small plant-eating dinosaur. It held its body horizontally and **ran fast** on its hind legs along the swampy shores. #0271

In China, 125 million years ago, the **Cretaceous swamp** was home to a dinosaur called **Dilong,** whose name means "Emperor Dragon." #0272

TWO-LEGGED *DILONG* LIVED IN THE SWAMPY LAND THAT IS NOW IN EASTERN ASIA. IT WAS THE FIRST TYRANNOSAUROID TO BE DISCOVERED WITH **FEATHERS.** #0273

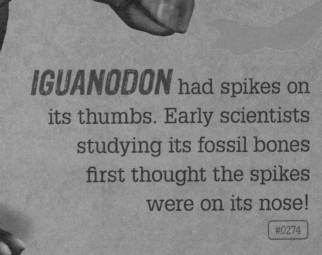

IGUANODON had spikes on its thumbs. Early scientists studying its fossil bones first thought the spikes were on its nose! #0274

71

6 FACTS ABOUT SWAMP FORESTS

The late **CRETACEOUS** swamp forests were full of plants, including the first flowers. #0275

Flowers may have been a vital food for **HUGE** herds of duckbill

HADROSAURS.
#0276

HADROSAURS used their mouths to clip off forest vegetation and their **many tiny teeth** to grind it down.
#0277

Agile theropods such as **TYRANNOSAURUS REX** may have lurked among the trees to ambush duckbill dinosaurs and other plant-eaters of the swamp forest.

#0278

TROODON probably ate other dinosaurs' eggs, small mammals, lizards, and invertebrates that lived in the Cretaceous swamp forests.

#0279

PARASAUROLOPHUS

had a head crest packed with hollow tubes, which probably helped it to signal by **trumpeting** to others in the herd as they moved through the forest.

#0280

73

7 FACTS ABOUT SHALLOW SEAS AND LAGOONS

During the **JURASSIC** and **CRETACEOUS,** shallow seas and great lagoons drew many dinosaurs to the water's edge.
#0281

Lagoons were separated from the sea by reefs and were ideal **fossil-forming** zones. #0282

NOTHOSAURUS was an early sea reptile with interlocking teeth that **SNAPPED** together to catch unsuspecting dinosaurs that came too close to the water's edge. #0283

When dinosaurs died in the water, they **sank** straight to the bottom and became **preserved** in the soft silt.
#0284

Pterosaur fossils, including **PTERODACTYLUS,** **RHAMPHORHYNCHUS,** and **ANUROGNATHUS,** were discovered in what was a salty lagoon in Solnhofen, Germany. #0285

ARCHAEOPTERYX and **COMPSOGNATHUS** lived on the shores of a lagoon in Solnhofen, Germany, around 150 million years ago. #0286

NOTHOSAURUS came ashore to lay eggs, but, if frightened, it went straight back to the safety of the lagoon. #0287

75

7 FACTS ABOUT SEASHORE HABITATS

When **coastal dinosaurs** died, their remains were washed into the sea, which helped to preserve them.

#0288

ROAMING along the coastline **millions of years ago** were ...

... meat-eating **theropods,**

... plant-eating dinosaurs,

... and early beaked dinosaurs.

#0289

ANKYLOSAURUS was one of the heavily armored dinosaurs that ambled along estuaries and coastlines 67 million years ago.

#0290

HUNGAROSAURUS was a heavily armored dinosaur that probably lived near the seashore. #0291

HUNGAROSAURUS fossils have been found next to those of **fish, crocodiles, and turtles.** #0292

PLANICOXA was a four-legged dinosaur that could rear up on its hind legs to reach leaves from shoreline trees. #0293

The remains of around **300,000 dinosaur eggs** were found at an ancient **seashore nesting site** in what is now northeastern Spain. #0294

8 FACTS ABOUT
OCEAN LIVING

Giant **ICHTHYOSAURS,** sea reptiles that looked like modern-day fish, ruled the oceans in the early Triassic, **240 million** years ago. #0295

Late in the Triassic, **205 million** years ago, the first **PLESIOSAURS** swam the ocean. #0296

Cymbospondylus was a sleek, powerful predator that grew up to **33 feet in length.** It was the **largest** ichthyosaur ever to have evolved. #0297

Liopleurodon, a pliosaur, was one of the largest ocean predators **of its time.** Scientists know from its **huge** nostrils that it had an extremely good sense of smell and would have been a **highly efficient predator.** #0298

Some **PLESIOSAURS'** necks contained **70** vertebrae—humans have only seven!

#0299

Archelon was a giant Cretaceous turtle with broad, powerful front flippers. It was one of the **biggest turtles ever.**

#0300

ARCHELON was 13 feet long and nearly 16 feet wide from flipper to flipper—the size of a small car!

#0301

When **Cretaceous** sea creatures died, their skeletons fell to the ocean floor and eventually became **chalk.**

#0302

FACTS ABOUT

8 ISLAND LIFE

After Earth's supercontinent, Pangaea, split up, the world's oceans, seas, and lakes became dotted with tiny islands.

#0303

DINOSAURS that lived on islands gradually evolved into much smaller "DWARF SPECIES" because of a lack of food.

#0304

PTEROSAURS lived in coastal areas, and some would have soared over the islands, swooping down to catch fish from the sea.

#0305

A small island could only support a small population of dinosaurs.

#0306

80

TELMATOSAURUS, a hadrosaur dinosaur, became a dwarf species on Hateg Island, which later became part of **Romania.**
#0307

Dinosaurs on islands had few large **predators.**
#0308

MAGYAROSAURUS was a relative of the giant **ARGENTINOSAURUS,** but because it lived on an island, it never grew larger than a horse. #0309

Ten-foot-long **STRUTHIOSAURUS** was an island-dwelling **"DWARF DINOSAUR"** that fed on shoreline plants. #0310

7 FACTS ABOUT POLAR DINOSAURS

North Pole

South Pole

In the **MESOZOIC ERA,** the Poles were warmer than they are today— around 32° Fahrenheit in winter and 68° Fahrenheit in summer.

#0311

The Poles were **DARK.** This was because the Sun did not rise for several **MONTHS** in the winter.

#0312

LEAELLYNASAURA had big eyes to see in the polar darkness and dug burrows to keep warm. #0313

Many fossilized **POLAR DINOSAUR** tracks made millions of years ago have been discovered in **AUSTRALIA.** #0314

Small-brained *MINMI* once lived near the South Pole in what is now **Queensland, Australia.** #0315

Scientists found what might be the **FOSSILIZED** remains of a last meal in part of a *MINMI* dinosaur's stomach. #0316

MINMI'S fossilized stomach contents included what may have been **twigs** or **stems,** bundles of **leaf tissues,** and **seeds.** This tells us about the plants it fed on near the South Pole! #0317

8 FACTS ABOUT DINOSAURS AND VOLCANOES

When a volcano **ERUPTED,** poisonous gas and fine, hot ash rained down, **KILLING** dinosaurs, other animals, and plants.

#0319

There were many more **VOLCANOES** during the Mesozoic Era than there are today.

#0318

Volcanic eruptions killed **MANY** dinosaurs, but the ash preserved their **nests, eggs, bones,** and **footprints.**

#0320

Vast layers of ancient volcanic ash in **China** preserved fossils of dinosaurs, such as **SHUVUUIA,** for millions of years.

#0321

Scientists can figure out the age of ANCIENT ASH, and from this, they can estimate how long ago dinosaurs lived.

#0322

Fossil bones from dinosaurs killed by volcanic eruptions contain fine **spiderweb cracks,** just like those of the human victims in Pompeii, Italy, when Mount Vesuvius **EXPLODED!**

#0323

Dinosaurs killed by one eruption in **China** died with their limbs stretched out.

#0324

Scientists **analyzed** rock in China's Liaoning Province and found around **24** fossilized young dinosaur skeletons. They found that the dinosaurs were probably caught in one **HUGE VOLCANIC EXPLOSION** of water, mud, and rock.

#0325

85

DINOSAUR HABITAT FACT FILE

A **desert sandstorm** could **KILL** a dinosaur, burying it in **tons** of sand.

#0326

Just like today, prehistoric deserts had **OASES** where dinosaurs would gather.

#0327

DINOSAURS NEEDED TO DRINK FROM LIFE-SAVING OASES BUT SOMETIMES GOT **SUCKED** INTO DEADLY **QUICKSAND.**

#0328

Water trapped behind **reefs** formed warm, shallow **LAGOONS,** but as the water evaporated, the salt grew ever more **dense** and became **TOXIC** to dinosaurs.

#0330

The bottoms of **LAGOONS** were poisonous, with little oxygen and lots of minerals. Prehistoric creatures that ended up in these murky depths did not last long.

#0331

SWARMS OF **INSECTS** LIVED NEAR THE LAKES WHERE THE REPTILES, **GREAT** AND small, SWAM AND HUNTED.

#0329

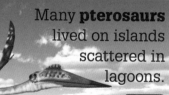

Many **pterosaurs** lived on islands scattered in lagoons.

#0332

The **CRETACEOUS PLAINS** were similar to the African plains today. Instead of zebras, great herds of dinosaurs **roamed** the land with **predators close behind.** #0333

Long-necked sauropods were the major plant-eaters throughout the **Jurassic.** #0334

Sauropods traveled through forests of **CONIFERS, GINKGOES,** and **TREE FERNS,** tramping from one thicket to another in **search of food.** #0335

Utah's Dinosaur National Monument was once a **riverbank forest** and home to many dinosaurs. #0336

Fossil bones of many **CENTROSAURUS** dinosaurs were found in **ALBERTA, CANADA.**

They may have been killed by a **HUGE** storm that flooded the coastal landscape. #0337

TAR PITS
WERE DEADLY. AS ONE ANIMAL FELL IN, OTHERS TRIED TO EAT IT AND WERE SOON ALSO TRAPPED. #0339

Lakes that formed in **DEEP RIFT VALLEYS** provided fresh water that supported a **GREAT** variety of life, such as mammals, fish, insects, and dinosaurs. #0341

FOSSILIZED DINOSAUR TRACKS reveal that dinosaurs migrated for **hundreds of miles** along beaches. #0338

As dinosaurs evolved, so did the **plants** they ate. Plants survived by their ability to scatter seeds that could grow even when the parent plant had been **swallowed up!** #0340

DINOSAUR
DIETS

Finding something to eat and not being **EATEN** took up most of the day for any plant-eating dinosaur. #0342

CHAPTER 4

9 FACTS ABOUT PLANT-EATERS

Scientists look at the fossilized teeth of each type of plant-eating dinosaur to find out whether it ate soft or tough plant material. #0343

The **LENGTH** of a plant-eater's neck helps reveal what type of leaves it ate ...

... the **LONGER** its neck, the **HIGHER** it could reach! #0344

Many peaceful plant-eaters had spikes, horns, and bumps that looked **FEROCIOUS**. #0345

MAMENCHISAURUS used its 36-foot neck to reach its food! #0346

STYRACOSAURUS had a head frill like an enormous collar. This helped to **protect** its **neck** from attacking meat-eaters. #0347

When **STEGOSAURUS** was nervous or angry, its backplates may have filled with blood, making them turn crimson. #0348

BARAPASAURUS, like other **sauropods,** had a **fermentation chamber** in its gut! #0349

A **fermentation chamber** helped dinosaurs to **process** tough plants. It contained **bacteria** that broke down plant material, making it easier to **digest.** #0350

Plant-eating sauropod dinosaurs probably produced lots of **GAS!** #0351

91

13 FACTS ABOUT DEADLY MEAT-EATERS

Meat-eating dinosaurs included the **RUTHLESS RAPTORS,** which had muscular jaws and grasping clawed hands. #0352

UTAHRAPTOR could probably smell prey from at least **a mile** away. #0354

Some raptors were as **small** as chickens; others were **taller** than a human being! #0353

TYRANNOSAURUS REX teeth could rip off up to **500** pounds of flesh in a **single bite!** #0355

The tiny dinosaur **PARVICURSOR** fed on **termites.** #0356

NEOVENATOR was a meat-eating dinosuar that **tore chunks** out of its prey. #0357

SKORPIOVENATOR
may have arched its head back then swung it down, driving its teeth into its prey's flesh. #0358

MAJUNGASAURUS ate sauropods—and each other! #0360

STOMATOSUCHUS was a **33-foot-long** crocodilian that lived alongside the dinosaurs. #0361

STOMATOSUCHUS competed with meat-eating dinosaurs, gulping small creatures into its pelicanlike pouch. #0362

Insects, lizards, and **turtles** were all food for dinosaurs. #0363

Dinosaurs often searched for meals that didn't fight back, such as **EGGS.** #0364

93

7 DINOSAUR ATTACKS

An attacking dinosaur may have **bitten, slashed,** or **knocked** down and **trampled** its prey. #0365

Two **Ankylosaurus** may have used their **tail clubs** in fights over territory or mates. #0366

VELOCIRAPTOR was FAST and AGILE. It could leap in the air and slash its prey using its sharp claws. #0367

To ward off ferocious meat-eaters, long-tailed sauropods, such as *Diplodocus*, may have **whipped** them with their long tails.

#0368

Attacking dinosaurs would single out the **young** or **weak** in a herd.

#0369

GIGANOTOSAURUS

was one of the largest meat-eating dinosaurs to ever thunder across the land.

#0370

One *GIGANOTOSAURUS* would have been terrifying, but these savage giants may have **hunted in packs.**

#0371

FACTS ABOUT
8 GRAZING DINOSAURS

The Jurassic landscape was full of dinosaurs that ate **mosses, ferns, horsetails, cycads, ginkgoes,** and **conifers.** #0372

Flowering plants first appeared 125 million years ago, which meant that late Cretaceous dinosaurs would have eaten **fruit.** #0373

The mouths of some plant-eaters, such as *PLATEOSAURUS,* were packed with **leaf-shaped** teeth. Other plant-eaters, such as *DIPLODOCUS,* had teeth that were long and thin and looked more like pencils. #0374

BLUNT TEETH
were great for **stripping** vegetation such as twigs and leaves. #0375

FLAT TEETH
could help to **grind** up tough plant fibers. #0376

Ankylosaurs had teeth designed for slicing plants, but not for chewing their food. #0377

Plant-eating **ORNITHOMIMUS'** name means **"bird mimic"** because it looks similar to a modern-day **OSTRICH** or **EMU.** #0378

ORNITHOMIMUS mainly ate plants but also occasionally fed on **small animals.** #0379

12 FACTS ABOUT HOW NOT TO BE EATEN!

Many modern-day plant-eaters try to **blend** into the background, so some dinosaurs probably had **SPOTS** or **STRIPES**.
#0380

Fossilized skin is extremely rare and never keeps its color, so scientists cannot tell for sure if dinosaurs were **CAMOUFLAGED** or not. #0381

Dinosaurs did **NOT** want to be flipped over: Soft bellies were **vulnerable.** Being heavy with sturdy legs helped to avoid this.
#0382

TRICERATOPS three enormous horns and its almost 3-foot-wide frill helped defend it against attacks. #0383

If threatened, a group of **PROTOCERATOPS** stood in a circle around their babies or eggs to protect them. #0384

Thick skin gave **PINACOSAURUS** very useful protection. #0385

TALARURUS had thorny spikes on its back to ward off would-be attackers. #0386

STEGOCERAS' head was **40 times thicker** than a human skull. #0387

Head frills and spikes helped to protect **CHASMOSAURUS'** neck. #0388

Tough, **leathery skin** protected the dinosaurs from predators' bites ... #0389

... while **sharp horns** were able to pierce the thick skin of predators such as *Tyrannosaurus rex*. #0390

For some dinosaurs, the best strategy was to run away—

FAST!

#0391

9 FACTS ABOUT GASTROLITHS

Plant-eating dinosaurs **swallowed rocks** to help them digest their food. These rocks were called GASTROLITHS. #0392

Gastroliths helped to **GRIND UP** plant fibers inside the dinosaur. #0393

OMEISAURUS ate so much each day that it didn't have time to chew its food. Instead, it swallowed plants whole, and gastroliths did the work! #0394

A fossil gastrolith from a dinosaur can weigh several pounds. #0395

Some gastroliths found near sauropod skeletons are about **4 INCHES** long. #0396

100

Gastroliths probably **ROLLED** and **TUMBLED** in the digestive tract, sinking low down and grinding the food like a mill.

#0397

PLESIOSAURS may have swallowed **gastroliths** to counteract buoyancy and help them stay down in the water.

#0398

Minerals in gastroliths may have been a **USEFUL DIET SUPPLEMENT.**

#0399

Modern-day **animals**, such as **crocodiles, alligators, seals**, and **sea lions**, swallow gastroliths.

#0400

101

11 FACTS ABOUT THE DINOSAUR FOOD CHAIN

There were three layers in the dinosaur food chain: primary producers, **primary** consumers, and **secondary** consumers.
#0401

The **dinosaur food chain** started with plants and ended with **MEAT-EATERS.** #0402

Plants were primary producers. They thrived if there was **plenty of rain and sunshine.**
#0403

PLANT-EATERS were the primary consumers. They grew **plump** by eating lots of plants. This, then made them **good to eat.** #0404

Meat-eaters, such as **TYRANNOSAURUS REX** and **Utahraptor,** were secondary consumers. They ate any plant-eating dinosaurs they could catch. #0405

DINOSAUR DROPPINGS helped fertilize the soil so **plants grew.** This made more food for plant-eating dinosaurs in the dinosaur food chain.
#0406

If there were **too many meat-eating dinosaurs,** and they ate **too many plant-eating dinosaurs,** it became harder for the meat-eating dinosaurs to

FIND ENOUGH PREY.

#0407

Dinosaur life was a balancing act. A group of large herbivores grazing and munching needed thousands of acres of plants to survive and

G-R-O-W.

#0408

If plant food became scarce,

PLANT-EATING DINOSAURS

starved and died.

#0409

If plant-eating dinosaur numbers **dropped,** **MEAT-EATING** dinosaurs **DIED,** and their numbers dropped, too.

#0410

Dinosaur eggs were part of a food chain. Early mammals and

LIZARDS FEASTED ON THEM!

#0411

103

DINOSAUR DIET
FACT FILE

To find out what **dinosaurs ate,** researchers **STUDY THEIR SKULLS, teeth and jaws,** fossilized **stomach contents,** and **DINOSAUR POO.** #0412

BARYONYX had **96 TEETH,** many more than its fellow theropod, *Tyrannosaurus rex,* which had only **60 TEETH.** #0414

Baryonyx's jaws were **ANGLED** to keep its **FISHY** meal from wriggling out. #0415

BARYONYX hooked fish out of the water

with its **clawed thumb.** #0413

The name **OVIRAPTOR** means **"EGG HUNTER."** #0416

When the first **OVIRAPTOR** was discovered, it was surrounded by lots of eggs. Scientists later realized it wasn't **eating** the eggs but **protecting** its young! #0417

OVIRAPTOR had no teeth but a birdlike beak and **REALLY POWERFUL JAWS** so it could crush …

… NUTS,

… SHELLFISH,

… AND INSECTS. #0418

OMNIVORES WERE **UNFUSSY** AND ATE BOTH **MEAT** AND **PLANTS!**

#0419

Recent discoveries suggest that **SPINOSAURUS** may have waded through water to hunt for **fish.**

#0420

About **65 PERCENT** of dinosaurs ate only plants

35 PERCENT were meat-eaters or ominvores.

#0421

TYRANNOSAURUS REX ate meat and so did the **great majority** of its closest relatives, such as *oviraptor* and the dromaeosaurs.

#0422

Among the smallest meat-eaters was cat-sized **HESPERONYCHUS** at only **24 TO 32** inches long.

#0423

HESPERONYCHUS probably ate ...

... **INSECTS,**

... **SMALL MAMMALS,**

... **LIZARDS,**

... AND **BABY DINOSAURS.**

Tiny **COELUROSAURS** probably ate tiny **lizards.**

#0424

#0425

DINOSAUR
BEHAVIOR

Scientists study **living birds** to give them an amazing **INSIGHT** into the lives of the dinosaurs, millions of years ago. #0426

CHAPTER 5

10 FACTS ABOUT DINOSAUR EGGS

As far as we know, **ALL** dinosaurs laid eggs.

#0427

Big dinosaurs, such as *GIGANTORAPTOR*, laid eggs in small pits, and may have covered them in earth and leaves. #0428

Small dinosaurs may have sat on eggs to keep them warm, **just like hens do.**

#0429

Big dinosaurs could not have sat on their eggs without **SMASHING them to pieces!**

#0430

Feathered dinosaurs, such as **CITIPATI,** #0431 spread their long, feathered arms over their eggs to make sure they were **snug and warm.**

Up to
40
eggs have been found
in a **SINGLE NEST.**
#0432

Most dinosaur
eggs had
HARD, BRITTLE
shells, similar
to modern-day
birds' eggs.
#0433

Some dinosaurs
simply left their
eggs in the heat
of the sun to
**HATCH ON
THEIR OWN.**
#0434

The **LARGEST**
dinosaur eggs
were as big as
BASKETBALLS.
#0435

Shells from the largest dinosaur eggs
were up to **0.2** inches thick.   #0436

109

FACTS ABOUT
DINOSAUR FAMILIES

Dinosaurs laid **LOTS OF EGGS**, so that at least one hatchling would survive to reach adulthood.

#0437

Some **dinosaur families** may have lived together in herds, **nesting together**, caring for their young, and **KEEPING A LOOKOUT FOR DANGER.**

#0438

Being part of a group offered greater safety. Large herds could

STAMPEDE

and fend off predators when

ATTACKED.

#0439

Many young **hatchling dinosaurs** had to look after themselves the moment they **popped** out of the egg. #0440

A nest of **15 FOSSILIZED** *Protoceratops* babies was found in Mongolia, which suggests they were **growing up together,** perhaps watched over by a parent.

#0441

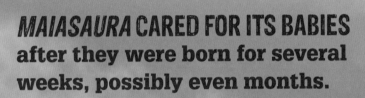

MAIASAURA CARED FOR ITS BABIES after they were born for several weeks, possibly even months.

#0442

Tiny baby sauropods were probably safer coping on their own when they hatched from their eggs—**away from their parents'**

BIG FEET.

#0443

8 FACTS ABOUT FIGHTS!

Some dinosaurs **fought to protect** their babies and their **eggs.**

#0444

DINOSAURS attacked **THEIR PREY** either singly or with others **in a pack.**

#0445

Megaraptor defended itself by **LASHING OUT** with its **sharp claws.**

#0446

Spring may have been a time of **FIERCE BATTLES,** when male dinosaurs fought for the attention of females.

#0447

Pachycephalosaurus
most likely
HEAD-BUTTED
the flanks (sides) of
its opponent's body.

#0449

Pachycephalosaurus
may have used the
bony dome on the
top of its head
for head-butting
rivals and enemies.

#0448

PACHYCEPHALOSAURUS
charged its attackers,
running at them
in quick, short
bursts of energy.

#0451

DINOSAURS
fought over
FOOD and **LAND,**
especially when there
wasn't enough of either.

#0450

113

FACTS ABOUT
WINNING DINOSAURS

8

The animals that were hunted evolved to run **REALLY FAST** to escape, then the hunters evolved to **RUN EVEN FASTER.** #0452

MASSIVE *Tyrannosaurus rex* and other **big meat-eaters** were so huge, they they could stun a victim by knocking it down to the ground before moving in for the **final kill.** #0453

A duckbill dinosaur fossil was discovered with a healed wound, probably from a *Tyrannosaurus rex.*

This showed it had fought #0454 against its attacker and **won!**

Graciliraptor's **small** size and light weight helped it to run from attackers. It was probably one of the **fastest** raptors. #0455

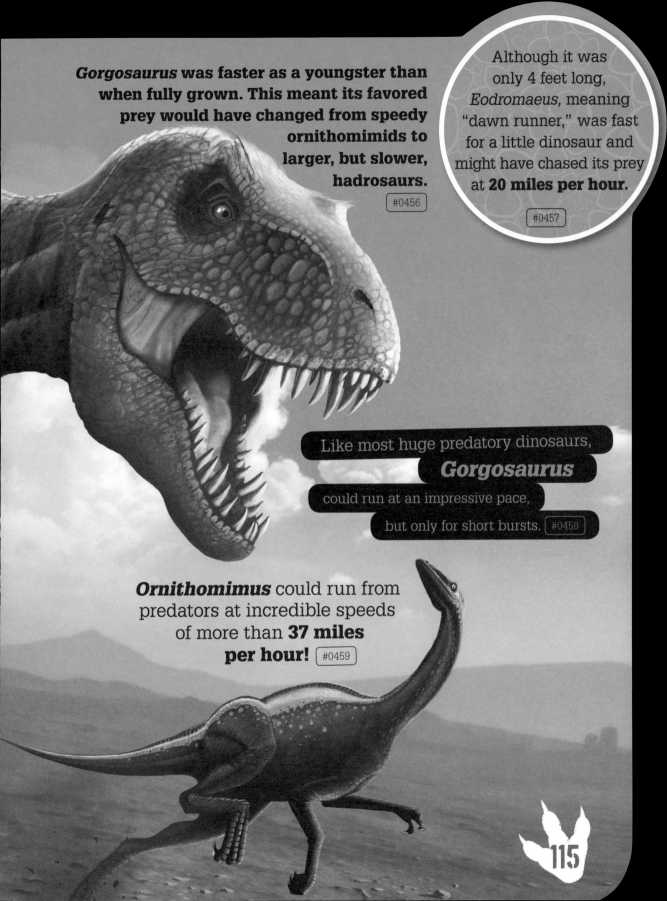

Gorgosaurus was faster as a youngster than when fully grown. This meant its favored prey would have changed from speedy ornithomimids to larger, but slower, hadrosaurs. #0456

Although it was only 4 feet long, *Eodromaeus*, meaning "dawn runner," was fast for a little dinosaur and might have chased its prey at **20 miles per hour.**

#0457

Like most huge predatory dinosaurs, *Gorgosaurus* could run at an impressive pace, but only for short bursts. #0458

Ornithomimus could run from predators at incredible speeds of more than **37 miles per hour!** #0459

9 FACTS ABOUT
DINOSAUR COMMUNICATION

Dinosaurs were **NOISY,** but it's been more than 66 million years since they were last heard on Earth! #0460

Scientists believe that dinosaurs communicated using **body movements and sound** because that's how **modern-day birds** and **reptiles COMMUNICATE.** #0461

Soft tissues, such as **vocal chords,** don't survive as fossils. This makes it difficult to know exactly what noises dinosaurs may have made. #0462

The **WHIP-CRACKING** sound made by a **Barosaurus' tail** would have traveled long distances and may have attracted potential mates. #0463

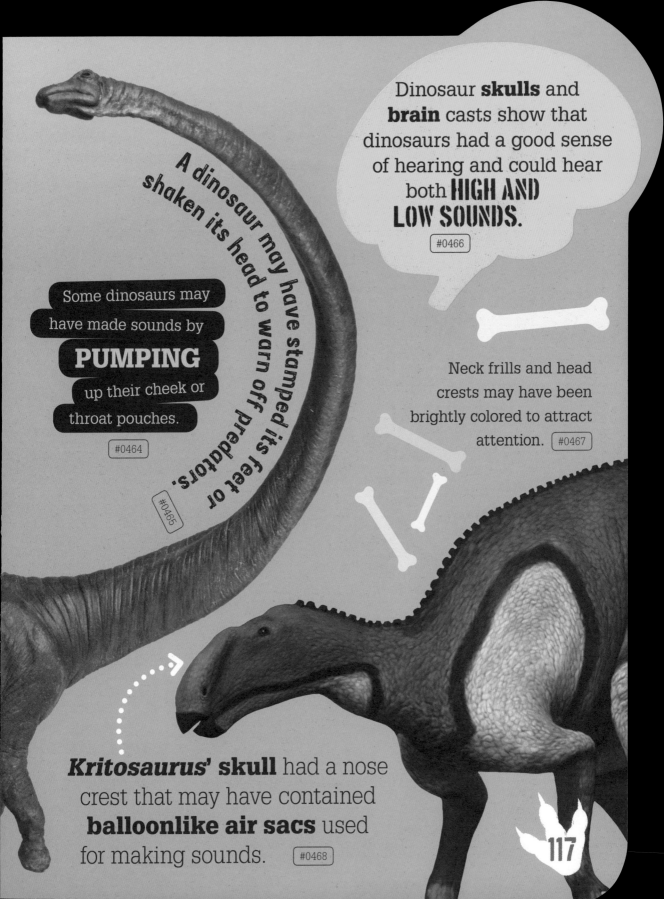

Dinosaur **skulls** and **brain** casts show that dinosaurs had a good sense of hearing and could hear both HIGH AND LOW SOUNDS.
#0466

A dinosaur may have stamped its feet or shaken its head to warn off predators.
#0465

Some dinosaurs may have made sounds by **PUMPING** up their cheek or throat pouches.
#0464

Neck frills and head crests may have been brightly colored to attract attention. #0467

Kritosaurus' skull had a nose crest that may have contained **balloonlike air sacs** used for making sounds. #0468

8 FACTS ABOUT
DINOSAURS AT REST

Many dinosaurs had no nest or burrow to rest in—they were constantly on the move.

#0469

A fossilized *Segisaurus* was found in what may have been a resting position, with its legs tucked beneath its body.

#0470

Fossils found in China, in 2007, tell us that some dinosaurs tucked themselves up, just like **modern-day birds.**

#0472

A fossil skeleton of a small, sleeping Chinese dinosaur fossil was named *Mei*, meaning **"sleeping soundly."**

#0471

DINOSAUR BURROWS

made by *Oryctodromeus*
have been found in Montana.

#0473

An ***ORYCTODROMEUS***
burrow reached about
20 INCHES
underground and
was just over
6.5 feet long.

#0474

Scientists studied **birds'** sleep patterns as a
way of speculating whether dinosaurs slept
or not. They think it probable that dinosaurs,
like birds, only slept for short spells.

#0475

Feathered dinosaur
Sinornithosaurus
was only active for
short periods of the
day and night in its
woodland home.

#0476

6 FACTS ABOUT
DINOSAURS ON THE MOVE

Gigantic pterosaurs may have flown long distances, perhaps **crossing** the **Atlantic**—which was about **186 MILES WIDE** in places—and flying over Eurasia. #0477

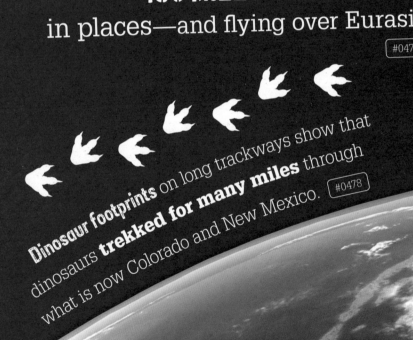

Dinosaur footprints on long trackways show that dinosaurs **trekked for many miles** through what is now Colorado and New Mexico. #0478

Plant-eating dinosaurs would have trekked along well-worn paths in pursuit of better food supplies,

FOLLOWED BY MEAT-EATERS. #0479

Analysis of **dinosaur teeth** shows changes in their make-up that suggest that sauropods, such as *Camarasaurus,* migrated during **the dry season.** #0480

The great dinosaur track that runs 400 miles through North America has been named the ...

DINOSAUR FREEWAY. #0481

Scientists think that as **dinosaurs evolved to be** B**IGGER,** **with longer legs,** they traveled farther to find food.

#0482

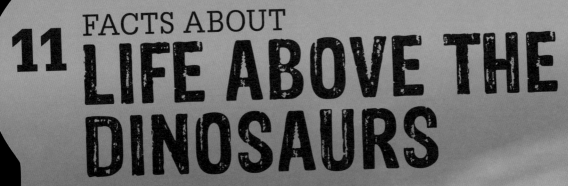

11 FACTS ABOUT
LIFE ABOVE THE DINOSAURS

PTEROSAURS were flying reptiles and the first creatures with a backbone to flap their wings and achieve powered flight. #0483

Although pterosaurs had light, hollow bones just like birds, they were only distantly related. #0484

There is no such animal as a **pterodactyl,** although lots of people use this name! There is a type of dinosaur called *Pterodactylus*, which belongs to the group called **pterosaurs.** #0485

Pteranodon had a **BACKWARD-POINTING** skull crest, which may have been used to **attract a mate.** #0486

A pterosaur's wing stretched from **its very, very long fourth finger.** #0487

When **pterosaur fossils** were first discovered, it was suggested that pterosaurs might have **glided** like flying squirrels or **swum** like penguins. We now know that they **FLEW.** #0488

FOSSIL DISCOVERIES

tell us that young and old pterosaurs may have lived together in large social groups.

#0489

PTEROSAURS

may have buried their eggs on #0490 shorelines.

Pterosaurs died out at the end of the Triassic. #0491

A PTEROSAUR had a large, leathery membrane stretched tautly between its body and long fourth finger. #0492

The largest Pteranodon had an **IMMENSE WINGSPAN** of up to **23 FEET,** which is as big as a small plane. #0493

123

RECORD-BREAKER
FACT FILE

NYASASAURUS

MAY BE THE **FIRST** DINOSAUR THAT EVER EXISTED. **It lived around** **243 million years ago,** which is 10 to 15 million years before dinosaurs were thought to exist!

#0494

EORAPTOR

HELD THE **OLDEST** DINOSAUR TITLE FROM 1993 TO 1999.

THIS DOG-SIZED SPRINTER IS **228 TO 231 MILLION YEARS OLD.**

#0495

DROMICEIOMIMUS

WAS ONE OF THE **FASTEST** DINOSAURS, RUNNING UP TO **43 MILES** PER HOUR TO ESCAPE **HUNGRY THEROPODS**.

#0496

One of the **smartest** dinosaur hunters included **speedy** *Troodon* with its brilliant vision, fine hearing, acrobatic agility, and balance.

#0498

The **oldest** known dinosaur fossil to be found in the United Kingdom is of a **210-million-year-old** *Thecodontosaurus*. #0497

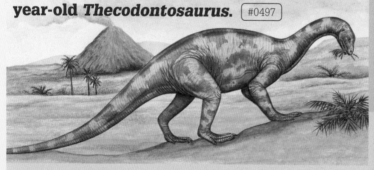

DEINOCHEIRUS had the LONGEST ARMS of any dinosaur—they were 8 FEET long! #0499

HUNTING IN THE ARCTIC CIRCLE

was a dinosaur called *Nanuqsaurus*. It may have been the **hardiest** dinosaur and was named after the local word for polar bear, "*nanuq.*"

#0501

The LONGEST dinosaur name is **MICROPACHYCEPHALOSAURUS!**

#0500

THE FIRST DINOSAUR REMAINS TO BE DISCOVERED IN THE UNITED STATES were found in 1854. The discovery included teeth from three dinosaurs: *TRACHODON, TROODON, AND DEINODON.* #0502

One of the most common fossil dinosaur skeletons found is that of parrot-beaked *Psittacosaurus.*

#0503

THE MOST DINOSAUR SKELETONS EVER TO DISAPPEAR WERE 18 THAT WERE snatched from Mongolia over a long period of time and returned home by the United States in 2014. #0504

Hundreds of **COELOPHYSIS SKELETONS,** THE **MOST** EVER FOUND TOGETHER, were found in 1947 in **NEW MEXICO**. The dinosaurs probably died of thirst at a dried-up water source before being buried in a flash flood. #0505

THE MIGHTY STEGOSAURUS ...

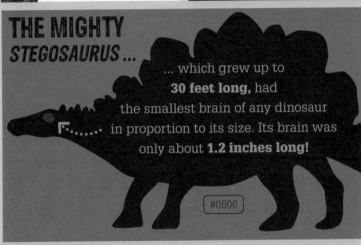

... which grew up to **30 feet long,** had the smallest brain of any dinosaur in proportion to its size. Its brain was only about **1.2 inches long!** #0506

The **shortest dinosaur name** is now shared by *Mei, Kol,* and the recently discovered *Zby.* #0507

The **LARGEST PLIOSAUR** was probably *60 feet long.* #0508

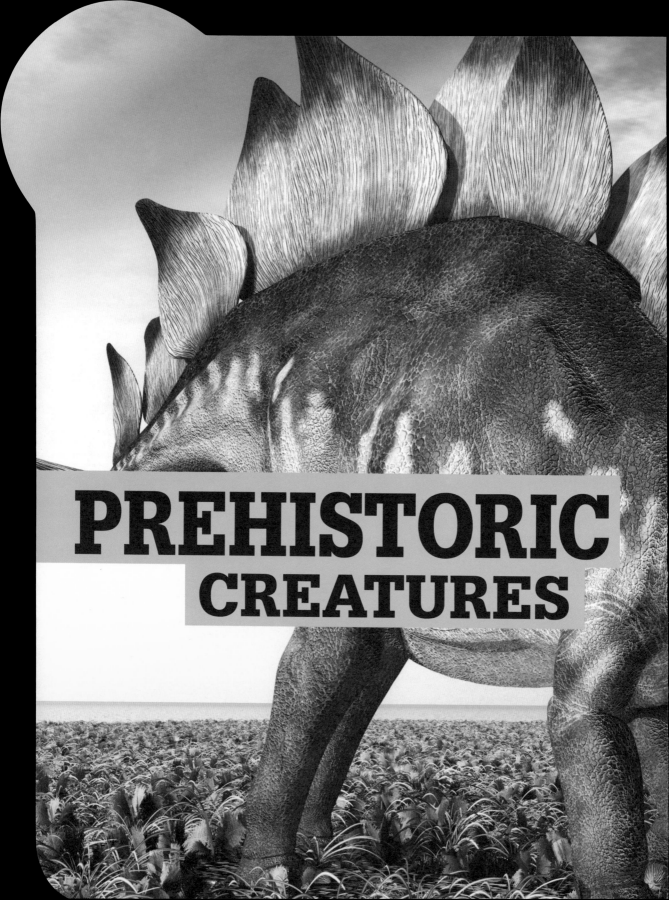

PREHISTORIC CREATURES

CHAPTER 6

Long ago, *Stegosaurus* munched on plants in subtropical forests ...

... **ABOUT 150 MILLION YEARS LATER,** **the world's most complete fossilized skeleton,** a *Stegosaurus* from Wyoming, was displayed in London's Natural History Museum.

#0509

Albertaceratops lived **80–75 MILLION YEARS AGO.** `#0510`

A **fossilized skull** belonging to *Albertaceratops* was found in 2001 in Alberta, Canada. `#0511`

Albertaceratops probably lived in a **large herd,** nibbling away at **small saplings and ferns.** `#0512`

Albertaceratops **had FIVE HORNS** on its head. `#0513`

Albertaceratops had unusually **l-o-n-g brow horns.** `#0514`

Albertaceratops was around **23 feet long.** `#0515`

Albertaceratops worked in groups to **fight** off **predators.** `#0516`

Albertosaurus lived **70 MILLION YEARS AGO.** #0518

Albertosaurus may have grown to a **LENGTH OF 33 FEET.** #0519

An adult Albertosaurus usually measured up to **30 FEET LONG.** #0517

Albertosaurus was a meat-eater with a **MASSIVE** head. #0520

Albertosaurus had **two horns** in front of its eyes. #0521

Albertosaurus had about 60 huge conical-shaped **SHARP TEETH** in its scissorlike jaws. #0522

The first **Albertosaurus skeleton was found in 1884.** #0523

Albertosaurus had only **two fingers** at the end of its **short arms.** #0524

Twenty-six fossil skeletons belonging to Albertosaurus were found together. This suggests they **hunted** in **packs.** #0525

ALLOSAURUS

Allosaurus roamed across plains, woodlands, and wetland shores **150 MILLION YEARS AGO.** #0526

ALLOSAURUS FOSSILS have been found in the **United States** and **Portugal.** #0527

Just like a tiger, meat-eating Allosaurus probably hid, **LYING IN WAIT** for its prey. #0528

Allosaurus could have leaped at least **10 FEET HIGH.** #0529

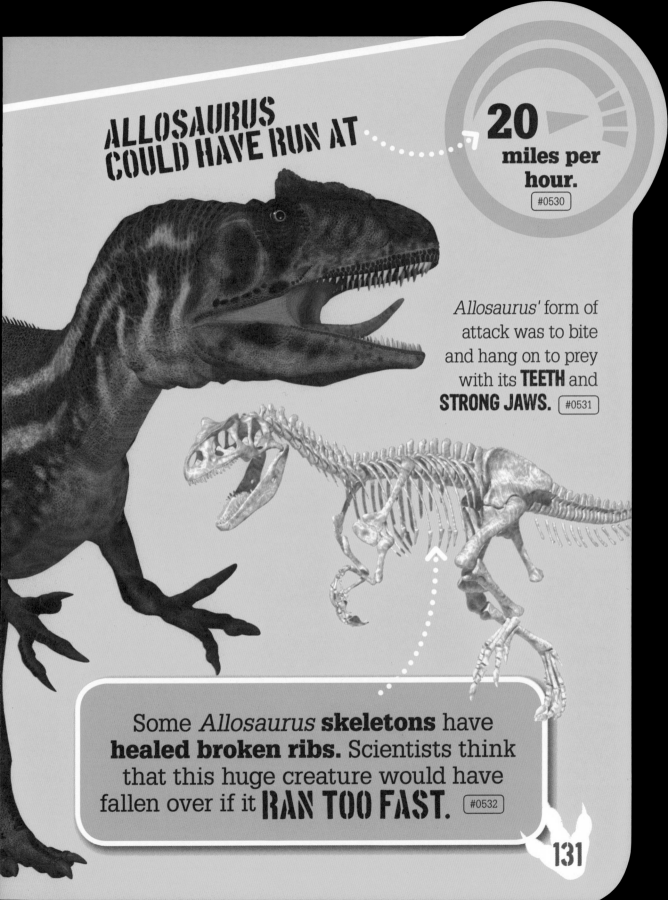

ALLOSAURUS COULD HAVE RUN AT

20 miles per hour.
#0530

Allosaurus' form of attack was to bite and hang on to prey with its **TEETH** and **STRONG JAWS.** #0531

Some *Allosaurus* **skeletons** have **healed broken ribs.** Scientists think that this huge creature would have fallen over if it **RAN TOO FAST.** #0532

9 FACTS ABOUT APATOSAURUS

Apatosaurus lived **147 to 137 million years ago.**

#0533

Apatosaurus lived in what is now **NORTH AMERICA.**

#0534

Apatosaurus was a **harmless giant** and one of the **LARGEST** land animals that has ever existed.

#0535

Apatosaurus used to be called **BRONTOSAURUS.**

#0536

Apatosaurus was **70 to 90 feet long** and **weighed 33 to 39 tons.** That's heavier than more than 400 men!

#0537

APATOSAURUS' NOSTRILS WERE ON THE TOP OF ITS HEAD. NO ONE KNOWS WHY! #0538

Fossil bones can get mixed up, and during one reconstruction, scientists put the **WRONG SKULL** on an *Apatosaurus* skeleton body. #0540

APATOSAURUS STOOD so TALL that predators could not reach to attack its head or neck. #0539

Fossilized *Apatosaurus* footprints tell us that tough pads covered its toes, just like those of modern-day elephants. #0541

133

7 FACTS ABOUT ARCHAEOPTERYX

DISCOVERED IN GERMANY IN 1861, *Archaeopteryx* had the **feathers of a bird,** with the **tail, teeth,** and **claws** of a **DINOSAUR.** #0542

Archaeopteryx had the coordination, balance, and vision needed to fly. #0543

Richard Owen, the creator of London's Natural History Museum, was the first to claim *Archaeopteryx* was a bird. #0545

Archaeopteryx is known as the **FIRST BIRD.** #0544

Archaeopteryx lived **150 million years ago**—previously, no birds were thought to exist that far back in time. #0546

Using a scanner, scientists built a three-dimensional model of *Archaeopteryx's* brain. #0547

Archaeopteryx's brain fitted so tightly into its head that it left an impression behind it on the skull. #0548

Brachiosaurus lived
153 MILLION YEARS AGO.
#0549

Brachiosaurus lived in what is now the **United States.**
#0550

Brachiosaurus was first thought to be one of the largest dinosaurs, but now **EVEN LARGER** dinosaurs, such as *Dreadnoughtus*, have been discovered.
#0551

Brachiosaurus may have been **WARM-BLOODED,** like birds and mammals are today.
#0552

It was **40 to 52 feet tall.**
#0553

In the **MESOZOIC ERA,** meat-eaters were less than half the size of *Brachiosaurus*. They probably **chased after easier prey,** leaving *Brachiosaurus* alone to **graze** in **peace.**
#0554

Scientists still do not know whether *Brachiosaurus* held its **LONG NECK** mostly vertically or horizontally, but it could probably **MOVE** between each **POSITION.**
#0555

8 FACTS ABOUT COMPSOGNATHUS

Compsognathus lived **150 MILLION YEARS AGO.** #0556

Compsognathus lived in the area that is now **Europe.** #0557

Compsognathus had a long **neck** and **tail** ...

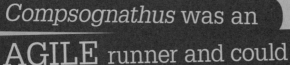

Compsognathus was an **AGILE** runner and could run at speeds of up to 39 miles per hour. #0559

Compsognathus' body was **no bigger** than a **chicken.**

#0560

... and was about **3 FEET IN LENGTH.**

#0558

Compsognathus was one of the first complete fossil skeletons **of any dinosaur to be found.**

#0561

A lizard has been found inside a **fossilized Compsognathus stomach.**

#0562

Compsognathus had a **large brain** for its body size and was probably among the more **intelligent** dinosaurs.

#0563

7 FACTS ABOUT DEINONYCHUS

Deinonychus lived about

115 to 110 MILLION YEARS AGO.

#0564

Deinonychus lived in the area that is now the **UNITED STATES.**

#0565

Meat-eating hunter *Deinonychus* grew up to

11 feet long.

#0566

Deinonychus' tail was stiff, which helped it to balance as it attacked prey.

#0567

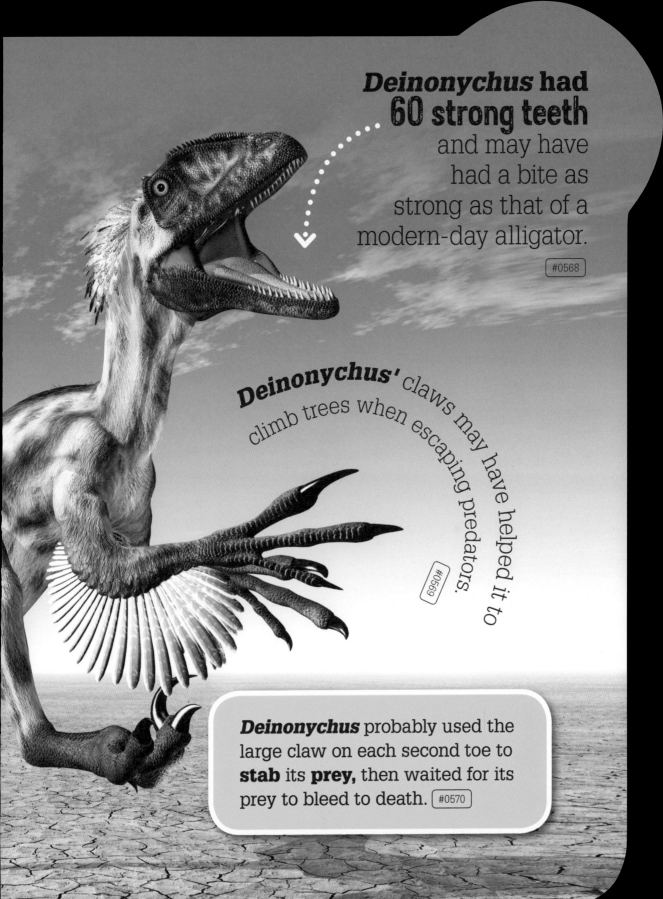

Deinonychus had 60 strong teeth and may have had a bite as strong as that of a modern-day alligator.

#0568

Deinonychus' claws may have helped it to climb trees when escaping predators.

#0569

Deinonychus probably used the large claw on each second toe to **stab** its **prey,** then waited for its prey to bleed to death. #0570

11 FACTS ABOUT DIPLODOCUS ON DISPLAY

A near-complete **_Diplodocus_ skeleton** was found in the United States in 1898.

#0571

It took **18 months** to make the **replica.**

#0573

When making the _Diplodocus_ replica, **missing bones** were cast from bones from four other specimens.

#0574

KING EDWARD VII had a _Diplodocus_ replica made for Great Britain.

#0572

King Edward VII's _Diplodocus_ replica was completed in 1904. It was shipped to Britain in

36 crates.

#0575

Britain's _Diplodocus_ replica was revealed in a special ceremony **on May 12, 1905.**

#0576

The _Diplodocus_ replica made for **King Edward VII** was the first **FULL REPLICA SKELETON** of a sauropod dinosaur to go **on display** in the world.

#0577

140

The *Diplodocus* replica became the **STAR EXHIBIT** in London's Natural History Museum. Its nickname is DIPPY. #0578

A total of **10 replica *Diplodocus*** skeletons have been made and sent across the world to different museums. #0579

A *Diplodocus* skeleton had **292 bones.** #0580

The *Diplodocus* replica has been **cleaned** every **two years.** #0581

14 FACTS ABOUT DREADNOUGHTUS

A *Dreadnoughtus* fossil was uncovered in Argentina between 2005 and 2009. #0582

Dreadnoughtus lived AROUND 77 TO 76 MILLION YEARS AGO. #0583

Its 36.7 foot neck was shaped like a **PIPE!** #0585

Dreadnoughtus is thought to have been the **heaviest** dinosaur ever. #0584

It took **five years** to excavate the colossal *Dreadnoughtus* fossil. #0586

Around **250 bones** from *Dreadnoughtus'* fossil skeleton have been recovered. #0587

Dreadnoughtus was probably **buried** when the ground turned to **quicksand** during a **flood.** #0588

Dreadnoughtus had a house-sized body weighing

nearly 66 tons

—as much as a herd of elephants. #0589

The **Dreadnoughtus** specimen that was found was not full-grown, so no one knows just how

ENORMOUS

the adults were. #0590

Dreadnoughtus was named after a type of **giant battleship.** #0592

Dreadnoughtus may have been buried so quickly by quicksand that **prowling scavengers** had no chance to **feast on its body.** #0591

The name *Dreadnoughtus* means

'FEARING NOTHING'. #0593

Dreadnoughtus had a muscular **29-foot-long tail.** #0594

Dreadnoughtus' **thigh bone** alone was as **long** as a **man** is **tall.** #0595

143

7 FACTS ABOUT DROMAEOSAURUS

Dromaeosaurus lived 75 MILLION YEARS AGO. #0596

Dromaeosaurus lived in what is now **North America.** #0597

Dromaeosaurus had **BIG EYES** and looked a little bit like an emu. #0598

Dromaeosaurus was about **6.5 FEET** long. #0599

Worn-down teeth suggest that Dromaeosaurus used its jaws for crushing and tearing. #0600

To **kill** its **prey,** Dromaeosaurus relied on its **powerful jaws** rather than its claws. #0601

Dromaeosaurus' bite was **MORE POWERFUL** than *Velociraptor's.* #0602

Gallimimus lived
70 MILLION YEARS AGO. #0603

One of the biggest chickenlike dinosaurs, *Gallimimus* was **20 FEET** in length. #0604

A **strong tail** gave *Gallimimus* **extra balance** and helped it to turn when **running quickly.** #0605

Some of the bones in a *Gallimimus* jaw were as thin as paper. #0606

The first ***Gallimimus*** fossil remains were found in the Gobi Desert in the early 1970s. #0607

Gallimimus had
HOLLOW
BONES
that kept it light. #0608

145

10 FACTS ABOUT
GIGANOTOSAURUS

Giganotosaurus roamed the Earth

100 TO 97 MILLION YEARS AGO

in swampland in an area that is now
South America. #0609

GIGANOTOSAURUS was a

HUGE MEAT-EATER.

#0610

**Weighing
9 to 11 tons,**
Giganotosaurus
was as heavy
as a male
**AFRICAN
ELEPHANT.**
#0611

Giganotosaurus
was an incredible
43 FEET LONG!
#0612

Giganotosaurus was so **BIG** and **STRONG**
that it probably could have **killed** some
of the **giant plant-eaters.** #0613

Giganotosaurus had a smaller brain than **Tyrannosaurus rex** but a massive skull. #0615

Giganotosaurus was **bigger** than Tyrannosaurus rex but more lightly built. #0614

One *Giganotosaurus* specimen was found near to fossils of some huge plant-eaters, possibly its prey. #0616

It had unusually **short arms.** #0617

Around 70 percent of a complete *Giganotosaurus* **skeleton** was found between 1993 and 1994. #0618

147

Giraffatitan lived **154 TO 142 MILLION YEARS AGO.** #0619

Giraffatitan was a huge **75-foot-long** stout-legged dinosaur. #0620

An incredible **34 individual Giraffatitan** fossils were found at a site in **Tanzania, Africa.** #0621

GIRAFFATITAN was discovered between 1909 and 1912, but was named *Brachiosaurus* by mistake. #0622

148

Giraffatitan means **"TITANIC GIRAFFE."** #0623

Gorgosaurus lived **75 MILLION YEARS AGO.** #0624

It may have been

an early relative of

TYRANNOSAURUS REX. #0625

The **fossilized tooth** of one *Gorgosaurus* has been found embedded in another *Gorgosaurus* jaw. They had **probably been fighting.**

#0626

Gorgosaurus' **scales were so small that its skin was almost smooth.**

#0627

Scientists found the fossil skeleton of one *Gorgosaurus* that had lived for months or even years with **FRACTURES, BROKEN RIBS,** an **INFECTED JAW,** and possibly a **BRAIN TUMOR!** #0628

149

Hadrosaurus lived 78 TO 74 MILLION YEARS AGO.
#0629

Hadrosaurus was 30 FEET LONG and could stand on either two or four legs.
#0630

Hadrosaurus fossils were discovered way back in 1838.
#0631

It was the **first dinosaur** to be identified from a fossil skeleton in the **United States.**
#0632

Hadrosaurus sometimes **ate rotting wood,** probably to consume the fungi and insects the wood contained.
#0633

In 1868, it became the **FIRST DINOSAUR SKELETON EVER DISPLAYED.**
#0634

Herrerasaurus was one of the earliest meat-eating dinosaurs to walk the planet—**231 MILLION YEARS AGO.** #0635

At the time of *Herrerasaurus*, dinosaurs were not the **TOP PREDATORS:** it would have had to run away from the giant forerunners of crocodiles. #0637

Herrerasaurus fossils have been found in Argentina's "Valley of the Moon"—a strange, barren place with a moonscape setting. #0636

Hererrasaurus walked on its **hind legs** and had **powerful, grasping** **CLAWED HANDS.** #0638

Its bladelike teeth were SHARP AND POINTED. #0639

Herrerasaurus was **10 TO 13 FEET LONG.** #0640

A hinge in its lower jaw helped it to keep a **FIRM GRIP ON STRUGGLING PREY.** #0641

FACTS ABOUT
8 IGUANODON

Iguanodon lived about
125 MILLION YEARS AGO. #0642

One of the most **successful dinosaurs,** *Iguanodon* lived in what is now Europe.
#0643

It was one of the **FIRST** nonbird dinosaurs ever **IDENTIFIED** from fossils and in, 1825 it was the **SECOND** to be given a formal name. #0644

Its name means
"IGUANA TOOTH." #0645

Iguanodon's teeth resemble those of an iguana (a type of lizard), but the dinosaur was

MUCH BIGGER

at about 33 feet long. #0646

The greatest number of *Iguanodon* fossils, **an AMAZING 35 to 40 skeletons,** was found in a Belgian coal mine in 1878. #0648

Iguanodon could easily walk either on

TWO LEGS OR FOUR. #0649

Mei lived around **125 MILLION YEARS AGO.** #0650

A fossil skeleton of *Mei* was found with its head tucked under its "wing," like a resting bird. #0652

Mei was discovered in **China, in 2004.** #0651

Mei was a feathered dinosaur with large eyes and a retractable claw on each foot. #0653

A small dinosaur, *Mei* was about the **size** of a **duck.** #0654

The living dinosaur may have been asleep when it was **KILLED BY POISONOUS GAS** from a volcano and **BURIED** in **ASH.** #0655

Nothosaurus lived **240 TO 210 MILLION YEARS AGO.** #0656

Nothosaurus probably **hunted shoals** of small **fish.** #0657

It was a

TRIASSIC SEA REPTILE. #0658

A **sleek swimmer**, Nothosaurus **swam** the seas around what is now **Asia**, **North Africa** and **Europe.** #0659

Nothosaurus had **WEBBED TOES.** #0660

Nothosaurus' long teeth fitted neatly together with its mouth closed. #0661

NOTHOSAURUS used its tail, legs, and feet to steer its 13-foot-long body through water. #0662

10 FACTS ABOUT
OVIRAPTOR

Oviraptor lived about
85 TO 75 MILLION YEARS AGO.
#0663

OVIRAPTOR WAS A SMALL DINOSAUR. IT WAS ONLY 6.5 feet long.
#0665

Oviraptor could **run 40 miles per hour** on its **two long legs.**
#0666

Oviraptor is only known from just **one** main **fossil specimen.** #0667

The *Oviraptor* fossil had a **crushed skull.** A *Protoceratops* may have caused this, since many *Protoceratops* fossils were found nearby.
#0668

Oviraptor's **parrotlike head** had a **toothless beak** but

POWERFUL, CRUSHING JAWS.

#0669

Its **beak** may have been used to **break open clam shells.**

#0670

The small **crest** on its **snout** may have **ATTRACTED** females.

#0671

Scientists think that *Oviraptor* probably had feathers like its close relative, *Citipati.*

#0672

157

In the early 1970s, a teacher in Canada discovered a site with **hundreds** of fossil *Pachyrhinosaurus* bones from **25 to 30 individual dinosaurs.** #0673

Pachyrhinosaurus measured up to **26 FEET** in length and weighed **4.4 TONS.** #0675

A herd of rhinoceroslike *Pachyrhinosaurus* may have **died in a flood 73 million years ago.** #0674

Pachyrhinosaurus is thought to have had **POOR HEARING.** #0676

Its **stubby teeth** were packed tightly together, slicing through plants like **pairs of scissors.** #0677

Pachyrhinosaurus is often found near fossils of the **duckbill dinosaur *Edmontosaurus*—this may** suggest that their herds traveled together. #0678

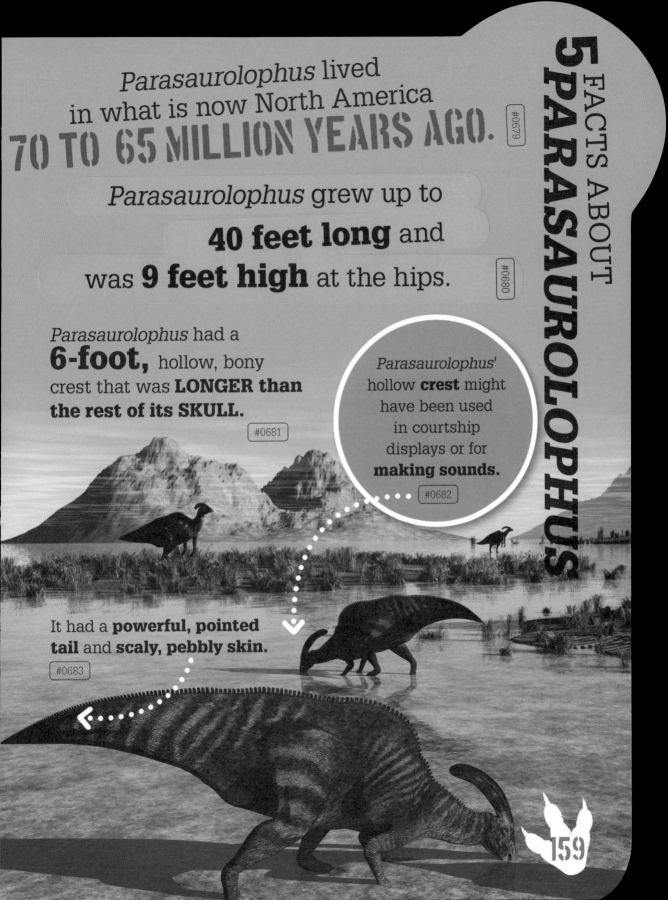

Parasaurolophus lived in what is now North America **70 TO 65 MILLION YEARS AGO.**
#0679

Parasaurolophus grew up to **40 feet long** and was **9 feet high** at the hips.
#0680

Parasaurolophus had a **6-foot,** hollow, bony crest that was **LONGER than the rest of its SKULL.**
#0681

Parasaurolophus' hollow **crest** might have been used in courtship displays or for **making sounds.**
#0682

It had a **powerful, pointed tail** and **scaly, pebbly skin.**
#0683

159

9 FACTS ABOUT PROTOCERATOPS

Protoceratops lived **75 MILLION YEARS AGO.** #0684

Protoceratops was a **plant-eater** about the size of a **sheep.** #0685

In 1922, an expedition looking for **early human fossils** in the Gobi Desert, Mongolia, discovered the **first Protoceratops.** #0686

Protoceratops was one of the **first dinosaurs** to be discovered by its **footprints.** #0687

In legends, **a griffin** is said to be **lion-size** with **big claws** and a **beak.** The legend may have been inspired by ancient **Protoceratops** discoveries. #0688

Protoceratops laid 12 to 15 eggs in its nest. Fossilized *Protoceratops* eggs have been found laid in a spiral pattern. #0689

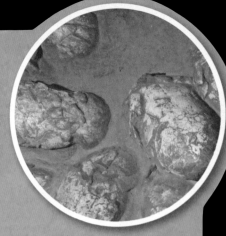

PROTOCERATOPS' JAWS WERE MUSCULAR AND PACKED FULL OF TEETH ABLE TO CHEW TOUGH VEGETATION. #0690

Some *Protoceratops* had small frills, but others had

ENORMOUS FRILLS **nearly half the length of their skull.** #0691

Scientists do not know whether **male** and **female** *Protoceratops* had different **frills,** or whether they have identified a **different type** of dinosaur. #0692

8 FACTS ABOUT QUETZALCOATLUS

Quetzalcoatlus is one of the **last-known pterosaurs** that survived to the very end of the Cretaceous, **66 MILLION YEARS AGO.**

#0693

It had two light yet enormous **16-foot-long wings.**

#0694

Like today's owls and eagles, it probably had **excellent eyesight** and could **spot prey** from **high** up in the **air.**

#0695

It was one of the **LARGEST FLYING ANIMALS** ever to exist. #0696

Quetzalcoatlus could glide **HIGH UP** in the air at **10,000 to 15,000 FEET,** and **SPEED** along at **75 miles per hour,** only occassionally flapping its wings.

#0697

When it landed and stood up on its **10-foot-long legs,** it looked a little like a modern-day giraffe.

#0698

Quetzalcoatlus probably **hunted land animals,** including small dinosaurs.

#0699

Some scientists wonder whether *Quetzalcoatlus* used its **strong front leg muscles** to vault into flight.

#0700

12 FACTS ABOUT
RAPTORS

Raptors were a group of **two-legged, meat-eating dinosaurs** with **feathered arms.** The scientific name for raptors is **DROMAEOSAURS.**

#0701

Scientists think that most adult raptors were **covered with feathers,** just like the hatchlings and juveniles were.

#0702

VELOCIRAPTOR lived **75 MILLION YEARS AGO.**

#0703

Microraptor lived **120 million years ago.**

#0704

Some raptors had a **HUGE, 9-inch-long,** curved **CLAW** on each hind foot.

#0705

MICRORAPTOR had **long feathers** on both its legs AND arms. It was a good glider, but its muscles were probably not strong enough to fly well. #0706

***Changyuraptor* lived 125 million years ago.** #0707

At just over **3 feet long,** *Changyuraptor* is the **BIGGEST** of all four-winged dinosaurs. #0708

Changyuraptor had **12-INCH-LONG TAIL FEATHERS** —the longest of any dinosaur. #0709

Utahraptor lived **126 million years ago.** #0710

Utahraptor was probably warm-blooded, which means it created its own body heat instead of relying on heat from the Sun. #0711

Named after the state of Utah, where it was discovered, *Utahraptor* was the LARGEST RAPTOR dinosaur that ever lived. #0712

9 FACTS ABOUT SAUROPOSEIDON

Sauroposeidon was a giant sauropod dinosaur that lived **110 million** years ago. `#0713`

SAUROPOSEIDON lived by river deltas on the shores of the Gulf of Mexico. `#0714`

SAUROPOSEIDON'S thigh bones are the **longest** of any dinosaur. `#0715`

Although **SAUROPOSEIDON'S** bones were big, they were full of tiny air pockets, which made them light. `#0716`

When fossil bones of **SAUROPOSEIDON** were first discovered in 1994, they were thought to be fossil **tree trunks!** `#0717`

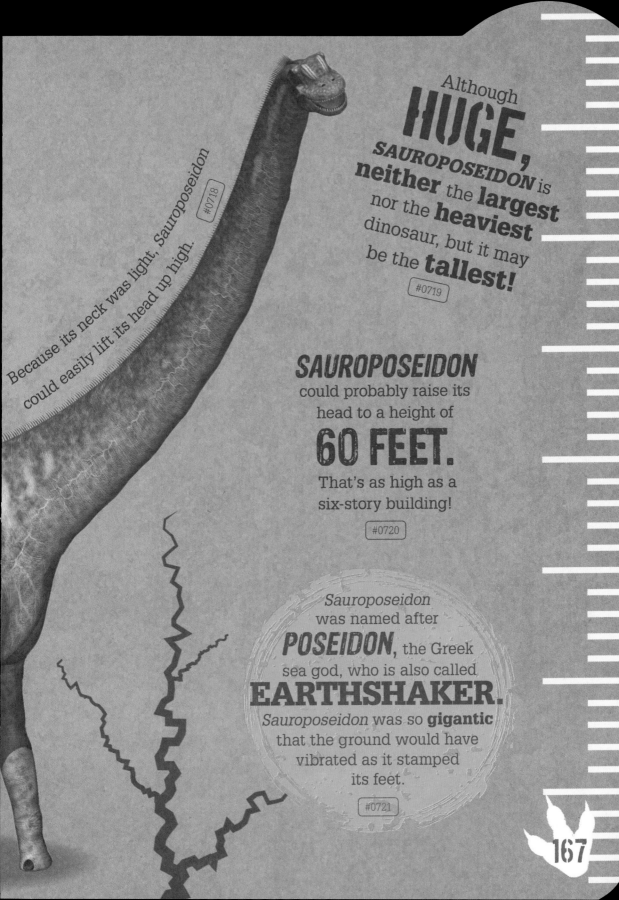

Because its neck was light, Sauroposeidon could easily lift its head up high.

#0718

Although **HUGE,** SAUROPOSEIDON is **neither** the **largest** nor the **heaviest** dinosaur, but it may be the **tallest!**

#0719

SAUROPOSEIDON could probably raise its head to a height of **60 FEET.** That's as high as a six-story building!

#0720

Sauroposeidon was named after **POSEIDON,** the Greek sea god, who is also called **EARTHSHAKER.** Sauroposeidon was so **gigantic** that the ground would have vibrated as it stamped its feet.

#0721

9 FACTS ABOUT SPINOSAURUS

Spinosaurus was a meat-eating dinosaur that lived 110 to 95 million years ago. #0722

Spinosaurus is the largest known land predator **of all time.** #0723

The first Spinosaurus fossil was found more than **100 years** ago, but a new fossil was discovered in 2013! #0724

The biggest **SPINOSAURUS** fossil was discovered in the Sahara Desert, Morocco. #0725

SPINOSAURUS had a **crocodilelike snout, paddlelike feet,** and **curved, bladelike claws** that hooked into its prey and sliced it up. #0726

SPINOSAURUS was as long as **two** buses! It was nearly 10 feet longer than any known **TYRANNOSAURUS REX**. #0727

SPINOSAURUS had a tall sail on its back.
#0728

SPINOSAURUS lived in swamp areas and probably hunted prehistoric crocodilians and fish.
#0729

Spinosaurus is probably the **FIRST** dinosaur identified as being able to swim.
#0730

169

6 FACTS ABOUT STEGOSAURUS

STEGOSAURUS roamed Earth **155 to 150 million** years ago in the late Jurassic. #0731

Stegosaurus lived in what is now modern-day western North America and Europe. #0732

STEGOSAURUS was the size of a **BUS** and had flat plates along its back. #0733

Stegosaurus held its tail high off the ground, but its head was held **LOW DOWN.** #0734

Stegosaurus weighed **5 TONS,** which is heavier than **six** cows! #0736

Stegosaurus ambled along slowly, eating **bushes** and **shrubs.** #0735

170

TRICERATOPS lived in the late Cretaceous around 68 to 66 million years ago. #0737

Triceratops' **ENORMOUS** skull, including its frill, could measure more than **7 feet** wide! #0738

TRICERATOPS was **30 feet** long and weighed **6.6** to **13 TONS.** #0739

Fossilized **TRICERATOPS** skulls are highly sought after and are bought for **hundreds of thousands of dollars** by dinosaur fans or museum collectors when auctioned. #0740

9 FACTS ABOUT
TROODON

Troodon lived **74 to 66** million years ago. `#0741`

Troodon lived in what is now the **UNITED STATES.** `#0742`

At 6.5 feet long, **TROODON** was a fast runner. It reached speeds of **25** miles per hour. `#0743`

TROODON LOOKED LIKE A BIRD AND MIGHT HAVE HAD **COLORFUL FEATHERS.** `#0744`

TROODON was **THREE** times heavier than **VELOCIRAPTOR** and **TWICE** its height! `#0745`

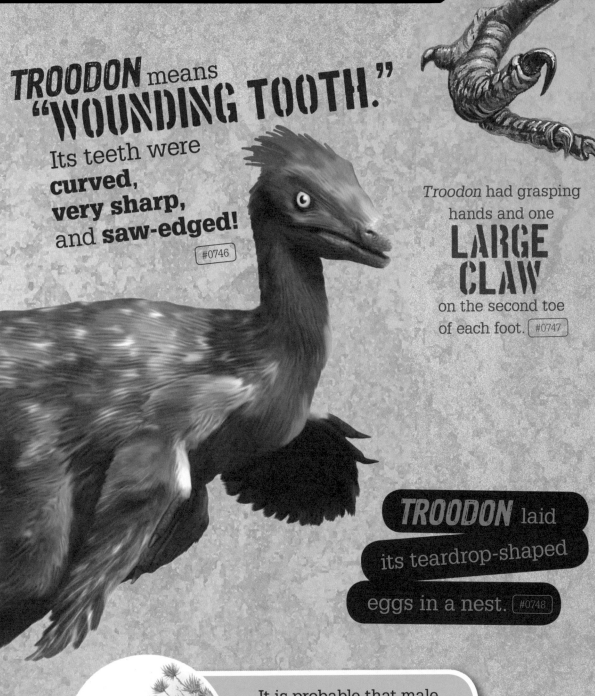

TROODON means **"WOUNDING TOOTH."**

Its teeth were **curved, very sharp,** and **saw-edged!** #0746

Troodon had grasping hands and one **LARGE CLAW** on the second toe of each foot. #0747

TROODON laid its teardrop-shaped eggs in a nest. #0748

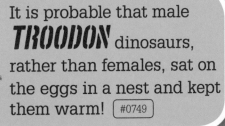

It is probable that male **TROODON** dinosaurs, rather than females, sat on the eggs in a nest and kept them warm! #0749

10 FACTS ABOUT TYRANNOSAURUS REX

Tyrannosaurus rex walked the Earth **67 to 66 million** years ago. #0750

Tyrannosaurus rex lived in what is now North America. #0751

Its jaws were so **POWERFUL** that *Tyrannosaurus rex* could slice right through its prey's head. #0752

Tyrannosaurus rex belonged to a dinosaur group called **TYRANNOSAURIDAE**, which also included: **ALBERTOSAURUS, ALECTROSAURUS, ALIORAMUS, DASPLETOSAURUS, EOTYRANNUS, GORGOSAURUS, NANOTYRANNUS, PRODEINODON,** and **TARBOSAURUS.** #0753

Its **BITE** had about three times the force of the bite of a **GREAT WHITE SHARK!** #0754

174

TYRANNOSAURUS REX was right at the **TOP** of the food chain— no predators dared to take it on! #0755

If prey bitten by *Tyrannosaurus rex* didn't die, it would have been left with **wounds** infected by **bacteria** that would kill it. #0757

Tyrannosaurus rex probably had very **BAD BREATH!** Pieces of dead meat may have gotten stuck in its teeth and would have **rotted** and **SMELLED TERRIBLE!** #0756

Traces of proteins in **TYRANNOSAURUS REX** bone closely match those of **CHICKENS!** #0758

Some **TYRANNOSAURUS REX** bones contain *Tyrannosaurus rex* tooth marks! This suggests it was either a **CANNIBAL** or fought with those of its own species for the attention of females. #0759

175

YANGCHUANOSAURUS lived 160 to 155 million years ago, in the mid to late Jurassic.
#0760

Yangchuanosaurus was a large, powerful **MEAT-EATER** that grew up to 30 feet long.
#0761

Yangchuanosaurus lived in what is now **CHINA.**
#0762

YANGCHUANOSAURUS had **BONY RIDGES** on top of its snout.
#0763

Its tail made up half its length.
#0764

Its huge skull grew up to **3 FEET** long.
#0765

YANGCHUANOSAURUS was similar in looks and size to the much better-known dinosaur, *Allosaurus.*
#0767

A construction worker in Sichuan Province, China, unearthed the first *Yangchuanosaurus* in the 1970s.
#0766

Only **two** main fossil skeletons of **YANGCHUANOSAURUS** have **ever** been found.
#0768

YUNNANOSAURUS lived **205 to 190 million years** ago, in the early Jurassic.
#0769

TWENTY YUNNANOSAURUS fossil skeletons have been discovered!
#0770

YUNNANOSAURUS was a long-necked plant-eater that roamed what is now **China.**
#0771

YUNNANOSAURUS was first named in 1942.
#0772

YUNNANOSAURUS HAD MORE THAN 60 SPOON-SHAPED TEETH.
#0773

YUNNANOSAURUS' teeth **sharpened themselves** by rubbing at each other as the dinosaur fed.
#0774

YUNNANOSAURUS was named after Yunnan Province, China, where it was first found.
#0775

Yunnanosaurus weighed up to **1 TON.**
#0776

Yunnanosaurus grew up to 23 feet long.
#0777

9 FACTS ABOUT
FLYING REPTILES

In 2014, a large fossil site was discovered in **BRAZIL.** It contained at least **47 PTEROSAUR** skeletons, now called **CAIUAJARA.** #0778

CAIUAJARA lived **85 million** years ago and had a head shaped like an old-fashioned **admiral's hat.** #0779

RHAMPHORHYNCHUS was a pterosaur that lived **150 million** years ago. #0780

RHAMPHORHYNCHUS had small legs, which probably made it a poor runner. #0781

RHAMPHORHYNCHUS caught prey in the water by snapping shut its needlelike teeth and then tossing the meal into its throat pouch, just like a modern-day pelican. #0782

A pterosaur named
HATZEGOPTERYX
flew over the Earth **68 TO 67 MILLION** years ago. #0783

HATZEGOPTERYX had a wingspan of more than **40 feet,** a huge 3-foot-long **beak,** and an **enormous** skull. #0784

HATZEGOPTERYX
lived on an island alongside dwarf dinosaurs. #0785

An early Cretaceous pterosaur called
TUPANDACTYLUS
had a sail-like head crest made of **BONE** and **KERATIN.** #0786

EXTREME PREHISTORIC
FACT FILE

Dinosaurs with the **LARGEST CLAWS** included …

… **MEGARAPTOR, THERIZINOSAURUS, BARYONYX, DEINOCHEIRUS,** and **SEGNOSAURUS.**

#0787

The pliosaur with the **LARGEST** appetite, swallowing **all** that swam in its way, was **KRONOSAURUS.** It ate large fish, turtles, and reptiles.

#0788

#0789

Two of the **MOST FEARSOME PREDATORS** included **SPINOSAURUS** and **MAPUSAURUS.**

SHANTUNGOSAURUS is the **LARGEST** duckbilled dinosaur so far discovered.

#0790

Two of the **BIGGEST PLIOSAURS** ever were **LIOPLEURODON**—a fierce marine predator at **20-36** feet long—and **KRONOSAURUS** at **30-33** feet long.

#0791

Some of the **SMALLEST** nonbird dinosaurs included **Compsognathus, Microraptor,** and **Mei.**

#0792

Predator X, now officially named **PLIOSAURUS FUNKEI,** was a vast pliosaur with one of the **MOST POWERFUL PREHISTORIC BITES**—four times stronger than **TYRANNOSAURUS REX!**

#0793

A dinosaur with one of the **MOST DIFFICULT NAMES** to say is *EUSTREPTOSPONDYLUS*. It is pronounced "yoo-STREP-toe-spon-DIE-lus."

#0794

Some of the **most well-armored** dinosaurs included *ANKYLOSAURUS, KENTROSAURUS, EUOPLOCEPHALUS,* and *SAUROPELTA.*

#0795

One of the **most well-protected** dinosaurs and the **most well-recognized** was *TRICERATOPS,* with its **MIGHTY ARMOR.**

#0796

The most **GIGANTIC MEAT-EATERS** included *CARCHARODONTOSAURUS,* which is closely related to *GIGANOTOSAURUS.*

#0797

Some of the most **gentle** giant browsers were *DIPLODOCUS* and *APATOSAURUS.*

#0798

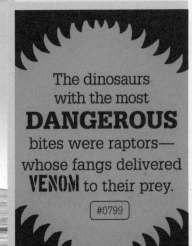

The dinosaurs with the most **DANGEROUS** bites were raptors—whose fangs delivered **VENOM** to their prey.

#0799

EXTINCTION AND BEYOND

Sixty-six million years ago, the world of the dinosaurs changed **FOREVER!** #0800

CHAPTER 7

11 FACTS ABOUT MASS EXTINCTIONS

A mass extinction is an event during which a large number of species die out in a short period of time. #0801

There have been **FIVE MAJOR** mass extinction events in Earth's history: two during the age of the dinosaurs; a small one at the end of the Triassic; and a larger one at the end of the Cretaceous. #0802

At the end of the Cretaceous, *66 MILLION YEARS AGO,* a **mass extinction** killed off the nonbird dinosaurs. #0803

Sixty-six million years ago, three-quarters of plant and animal species **disappeared.** #0804

In the Cretaceous extinction, **ammonites**, countless **flowering plants,** and **pterosaurs** perished. #0805

Some **INSECTIVORES** and **OMNIVORES** (creatures that ate almost anything) survived the mass extinction at the end of the Cretaceous, perhaps because there was more for them to eat. #0806

At the end of the Cretaceous, most land animals weighing more than

90 POUNDS

died. **BIG** animals need **LOTS** of food, and most of their food had **vanished.** #0807

Some **BIRDS** (also called **avian dinosaurs**) were **not** killed in the mass extinction. If they had been, they would **not** be around today! #0808

Big marine reptiles, such as **MOSASAURS, PLESIOSAURS, and PLIOSAURS,** disappeared from the oceans in the mass extinction, 66 million years ago. #0809

More than **80 percent** of Cretaceous **turtle** species **survived** the mass extinction. #0810

There were **more Cretaceous** survivors in the **sea** and in **fresh water** than on land. #0811

185

10 THE END OF THE DINOSAUR AGE

Many scientists think that a **massive** meteorite slammed into Earth, **66 million years ago,** ending the reign of the nonbird dinosaurs. #0812

METEORITES can be small or HUGE. #0814

A **METEORITE** is a piece of rock that travels from space and hits the Earth. #0813

Around **66 MILLION YEARS AGO,** the meteorite that hit Earth created the **Chicxulub crater** in **Mexico.** #0815

The **CHICXULUB CRATER** was discovered in the late 1970s. #0816

The **Chicxulub crater** cannot be seen. It was discovered by studying Earth's magnetism and rocks, and by oil-well drilling. #0817

186

The Chicxulub crater is more than **12 miles wide** and **112 miles deep.** The meteorite that caused it must have been at least **6 miles wide.**

#0818

The meteorite must have been traveling **120 times faster** than an airplane!

#0819

IRIDIUM is a metal found in meteorites. There is a layer of iridium on Earth that is **66 million years old**—formed by the meteorite that collided with Earth.

#0820

When a space object hits Earth, glassy, rocky particles form, called **tektites.** Scientists have found **66-million-year-old** tektites, which they believe were created by the meteorite.

#0821

8 FACTS ABOUT
THE DEADLY IMPACT

When the meteorite hit **EARTH,** the explosion would have created a **BILLION** times **MORE ENERGY** than the atom bombs dropped during World War II. #0822

Where the **METEORITE** hit Earth, the sky would have turned **RED HOT** for hours. #0823

In the crater's **impact area,** the surface of the Earth **baked** as if it was in an oven. #0824

The meteorite **IMPACT** would have been felt around the whole world. #0825

TOXIC GASES from the explosion filled the air, and **ACID RAIN** poured down on the dinosaurs.
#0826

The sea would have risen up into terrifying **MEGATSUNAMIS** flooding the land.
#0827

WILD FIRES raged on the land, **BURNING TREES, PLANTS, and ANIMALS,** including **DINOSAURS.**
#0828

SHOCK WAVES from the meteorite impact caused **earthquakes!**
#0829

189

8 FACTS ABOUT THE LAST DAYS OF THE DINOSAURS

Life after the meteorite impact was **dark.** Clouds of **debris, dust,** and **ash** blotted out the sun for months. #0830

When the sun was blocked out, plants **died** because they needed **sunlight** to survive. #0831

WITH HARDLY ANY SUNLIGHT, TEMPERATURES WOULD HAVE PLUMMETED—DINOSAURS COULD NOT SURVIVE THESE CHANGES. #0832

Plant-eating dinosaurs, such as huge **22-ton titanosaurs,** would have died out—they needed to eat **HUNDREDS** of pounds of vegetation every day and struggled to find a meal. #0833

The meteorite impact triggered **VOLCANIC ERUPTIONS**. Ash blocked out the sun and contributed to the mass extinction. #0834

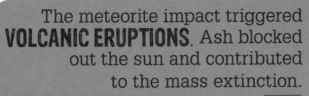

A meteorite impact may have caused the **sea levels** to change, destroying large areas of **DINOSAUR HABITAT.** #0835

Mighty tyrannosaurs and other meat-eaters had very little to eat once **VAST** numbers of plant-eating animals had died out. #0836

The movement of the **GREAT PLATES** that make up **EARTH'S SURFACE** could have also changed the climate and helped to **kill** off the big land **dinosaurs.** #0837

8 FACTS ABOUT
MASS EXTINCTION SURVIVORS

When the meteorite struck Earth, some underwater **sea, river,** and **lake** creatures were protected from the impact. #0838

Reptiles, including snakes, lizards, crocodilian and turtles, **SURVIVED** the mass extinction when the nonbird dinosaurs and other animals were **KILLED.** #0839

THE ONLY PLANTS TO SURVIVE WERE THOSE THAT WERE ABLE TO COPE WITH THE NEW **COLDER CLIMATE.** #0840

Amphibians such as salamanders and frogs survived the **MASS EXTINCTION.** #0841

THE ONLY DINOSAUR
SURVIVORS WERE
BIRDS.
#0842

FISH, STARFISH,
and SEA URCHINS
survived the mass
extinction. #0843

Mammals **thrived** once
there were no dinosaurs
around to compete for
land and food.
#0844

After the nonbird
dinosaurs became
EXTINCT,
mammals
became the
dominant
land animals.
#0845

FACT FILE

William Buckland was one of the first people to ever name a dinosaur. He named *MEGALOSAURUS* in 1824. #0846

Richard Owen, born in **1804,** was a clever **paleontologist, biologist,** and **anatomist.** #0847

Richard Owen realized that one fossil group, including *MEGALOSAURUS* and *IGUANODON,* all had columnlike upright legs, not sprawling reptile legs. #0849

Gideon Mantell was the world's first **DINOSAUR HUNTER.** In 1822, he was the first person to identify a dinosaur **tooth.** #0848

Richard Owen announced that the fossil bones he was examining were NOT LIZARDS AT ALL but something new —DINOSAURS. #0851

In 1842, Richard Owen gave the name **DINOSAURIA** to the strange fossils he was studying. #0852

Richard Owen was the **youngest ever** member of the **Zoological Society of London** in 1830. #0850

In the nineteenth century, Richard Owen studied new found **FOSSIL REPTILES** in Britain. #0853

Today's birds are dinosaurs, so even the BALD EAGLE (the United States' national symbol) and the ROBIN belong to dinosauria. #0854

As well as dinosaurs, Richard Owen studied **GIANT MOAS, KIWIS, AFRICAN LUNGFISH, GORILLAS,** and the **DODO** (an extinct bird).

#0855

Richard Owen gave biology lessons to the children of Britain's QUEEN VICTORIA.

#0856

Richard Owen noticed that an *IGUANODON* tooth had a totally different structure from an *IGUANA* (lizard) tooth.

#0857

#0859

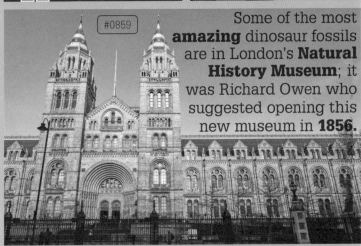

Some of the most **amazing** dinosaur fossils are in London's **Natural History Museum**; it was Richard Owen who suggested opening this new museum in **1856.**

It was Richard Owen's

GREAT RIVAL,

Thomas Huxley, who began to see the **links** between **dinosaurs** and **birds.**

#0858

The paleontologist **Robert Bakker** was one of the first to suggest that some dinosaurs had **feathers.**

#0860

In 1878, coal miners in Belgium discovered the remains of more than **30 DINOSAURS** in a deep ravine. **Louis Dollo** spent most of his life putting the skeletons **back together.**

#0861

Owen worked hard his whole life until the age of 85. #0862

Paul Sereno travels the world looking for **dinosaur fossils.** He found skeletons of *HERRERASAURUS* and *EORAPTOR* in South America and *AFROVENATOR, DELTADROMEUS, SUCHOMIMUS,* and *JOBARIA* in Africa.

#0863

FOSSILS AND DISCOVERY

People did not know that fossils were ANCIENT until the 1800s.

#0864

CHAPTER 8

14 FACTS ABOUT DINOSAUR FOSSILS

A fossil is the remains or **IMPRESSION** of a **PREHISTORIC** plant or animal, such as …

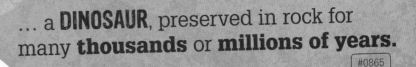

… a **DINOSAUR**, preserved in rock for many **thousands** or **millions of years.** #0865

It was **very rare** for a dead dinosaur to turn into a fossil. #0866

For a fossil to form, the first step was for the body of a creature to become buried by **SAND, MUD,** or **SILT.** #0867

Hard dinosaur parts that turned into fossils included **teeth, claws, horns, shells, droppings,** and **bones.** #0868

SOFT BODY PARTS OF A DEAD DINOSAUR WERE SOMETIMES **EATEN** OR JUST **ROTTED AWAY.** #0869

If hard dinosaur parts were buried by mud or silt, this soft rock eventually became **very hard.** #0870

Sometimes buried dinosaur bones were replaced **particle** by **particle** with ROCK. #0871

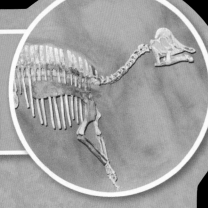

Buried dinosaur bones and other hard parts sometimes **DISSOLVED** over time when they were surrounded by rock, but their **shapes remained.** #0872

Underground shapes left by dissolved dinosaur bones became **filled** in with water **full** of **minerals.** The water hardened into **EXACTLY** the same **SHAPE** as the skeleton! #0873

Footprints, scratch marks, tail drag marks, and burrows have all been **fossilized.** #0875

As the top layers of rock wear away over **millions of years,** fossilized dinosaur bones and other hard dinosaur parts gradually **appear** at **EARTH'S SURFACE.** #0874

Fossils of **DINOSAUR FOOTPRINTS** tell us a lot about how heavy dinosaurs were, how they walked, and who was with them at the time. #0876

The earliest fossils date from **3.5 BILLION** years ago, way before dinosaurs existed. #0877

The most expensive dinosaur fossil ever sold was a *Tyrannosaurus rex* skeleton named "Sue." It sold for **$8.3 MILLION** in 1997. #0878

7 FACTS ABOUT FOSSIL HUNTING

The name fossil comes from the Latin word **FOSSILIS**, which means "obtained by digging." #0879

FOSSILS are often discovered where land has been disturbed by **construction works** or **coal mining.** #0880

FOSSILS ARE OFTEN FOUND WHEN THERE IS A ROCKFALL IN QUARRIES, ON FARMLAND, OR FROM CLIFFS. #0881

Fossils can be found in **MUDSTONE, LIMESTONE,** and **SANDSTONE** because these rocks are made of fine grains that settled on the dinosaurs' remains and buried them. #0882

Fossil hunters use **HAMMERS** and **CHISELS,** but the best tool is excellent **EYESIGHT** to spot **shapes** or **textures** in rock. #0883

A fossil may not be the same **color** as its surroundings if it has a different **mineral content.** #0884

A fossil might be just one tooth or egg, or a vast skeleton, such as that of a gigantic *DREADNOUGHTUS.* #0885

201

11 FACTS ABOUT FAMOUS FOSSIL HUNTERS

Mary Anning was one of the first fossil hunters and found many important fossils in the United Kingdom in the 1820s. #0886

Mary Anning may be the **GREATEST FOSSIL HUNTER** ever known. #0887

In 1903, **William Ferguson** found the first dinosaur fossil in Australia—a claw belonging to a meat-eating **theropod** dinosaur. #0888

In the early 1900s, Barnum Brown was chief fossil hunter for the **American Museum of Natural History.** #0889

Barnum Brown was the first fossil hunter to discover part of a *TYRANNOSAURUS REX* skeleton. #0890

Fossil hunter **Barnum Brown** sometimes used **DYNAMITE** to expose his dinosaur finds. #0891

Edwin H. Colbert discovered DOZENS of dinosaur fossils in the mid-1900s.

#0892

Edwin H. Colbert discovered **LYSTROSAURUS** fossils in Antarctica. This therapsid was also found in what is now South Africa.

#0893

Edwin H. Colbert's fossil discoveries helped prove that **AFRICA** and **ANTARCTICA** used to be joined together as one land mass.

#0894

José F. Bonaparte from South America discovered many dinosaur fossils, including **ARGENTINOSAURUS**, one of the **BIGGEST** that ever existed.

#0895

DONG ZHIMING has led numerous fossil-hunting expeditions in China and has named **20 dinosaurs.** He is called **"China's Mr Dinosaur."** #0896

39 FACTS ABOUT DINOSAUR NAMES

When a new dinosaur is found, the

PALEONTOLOGIST, RESEARCHER,

or its **DISCOVERER**

gets to choose its name. #0897

Some dinosaurs are named after the person who paid for the **fossil-hunting expedition.**
#0898

A DINOSAUR MIGHT BE NAMED AFTER THE PLACE IT WAS FOUND OR TO HONOR SOMEONE INVOLVED.
#0899

A dinosaur name may describe an **unusual feature** of the dinosaur, such as a big nose, or behavior, such as being fierce.
#0900

A dinosaur's name can also relate to **when it lived** or to a **famous event.**
#0901

ACANTHOPHOLIS:
spiny scales #0902

APATOSAURUS:
deceptive lizard #0903

BOROGOVIA:
named after the borogoves in Lewis Carroll's
poem "Jabberwocky" #0904

BRONTOMERUS:
thunder thigh #0905

BUGENASAURA:
large-cheeked lizard #0906

CARCHARODONTOSAURUS:
shark-tooth lizard #0907

COLEPIOCEPHALE:
knucklehead #0908

CORYTHOSAURUS:
Helmet lizard #0909

CRICHTONSAURUS:
Crichton's lizard (to honor Michael Chrichton,
the author of Jurassic Park) #0910

CRYOLOPHOSAURUS:
cold-crested lizard #0911

DASPLETOSAURUS:
frightful lizard #0912

DRACOREX:
dragon king #0913

DRYPTOSAURUS:
tearing lizard #0914

EKRIXINATOSAURUS:
explosion-born lizard #0915

EORAPTOR:
dawn thief #0916

GALLIMIMUS:
chicken (or rooster) mimic #0917

HAGRYPHUS:
Ha's griffin (Ha was an Egyptian god) #0918

IRRITATOR CHALLENGERI:
in honor of Professor Challenger in
Arthur Conan Doyle's book, *The Lost World* #0919

LYTHRONAX:
gore king #0920

MICROPACHYCEPHALOSAURUS:
tiny, thick-headed lizard #0921

NOTHRONYCHUS:
slothlike claw #0922

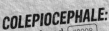

ORYCTODROMEUS:
digging runner #0923

QUAESITOSAURUS:
extraordinary lizard #0924

RUGOPS:
wrinkle face #0925

SALTOPUS:
hopping foot #0926

SKORPIOVENATOR:
scorpion hunter #0927

STYGIMOLOCH:
demon from the river Styx #0928

SUPERSAURUS:
superlizard #0929

TARASCOSAURUS:
Spanish dragon lizard #0930

TERATOPHONEUS:
monstrous murderer #0931

TITANOCERATOPS:
titan-horned face #0932

TRICERATOPS:
three-horned face #0933

VELOCIRAPTOR:
speedy thief #0934

VULCANODON:
volcano tooth #0935

205

13 FACTS ABOUT PREHISTORIC MISTAKES

Fossil dinosaurs are sometimes put together **incorrectly!** #0936

Dinosaur illustrations used to be only drawn with green or brown skin. We now know that some nonbird dinosaurs had feathers that were bright red or orange. #0938

Archaeoraptor was a **fake dinosaur,** made of two separate fossils put together. #0937

Fossil bones from **different** dinosaurs have been put together as **one** dinosaur. #0939

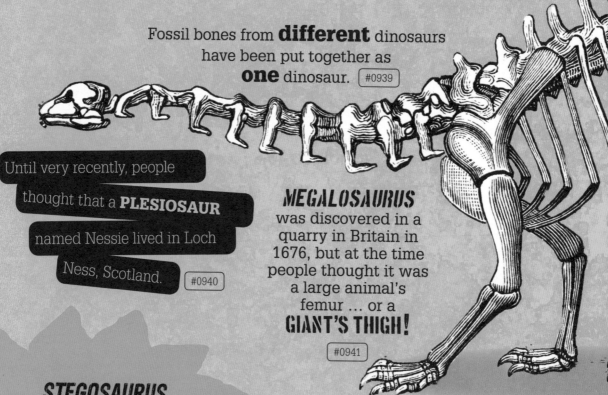

Until very recently, people thought that a **PLESIOSAUR** named Nessie lived in Loch Ness, Scotland. #0940

MEGALOSAURUS was discovered in a quarry in Britain in 1676, but at the time people thought it was a large animal's femur ... or a **GIANT'S THIGH!** #0941

STEGOSAURUS was once thought to have a second brain in its rump! #0942

The name **GORGOSAURUS** was "dropped" when its fossils were thought to be a young **ALBERTOSAURUS.** Many years later, fossils proved that these two dinosaurs were different after all, and the name **GORGOSAURUS** was reclaimed! #0943

In the 1800s, paleontologist O. C. Marsh thought that a **TRICERATOPS** skull, complete with horns, was from a **BISON!**

#0944

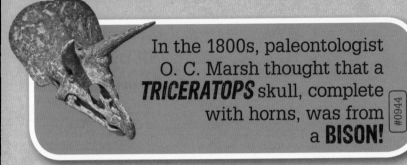

People used to think that dead dinosaurs **EXPLODED** when gas built up inside them.

#0945

In 1868, an excited Edward D. Cope put together a plesiosaur, **ELASMOSAURUS,** using fossilized bones, but he placed the skull on the **wrong** end of the skeleton!

#0946

People used to think that **BRACHIOSAURUS** lived in **water** and breathed with a type of **snorkel.**

#0947

Cavemen did **not** fight dinosaurs as shown in many movies and cartoons. There were more than **65.8 MILLION YEARS** between the last dinosaurs and modern humans.

#0948

207

13 FACTS ABOUT MESOZOIC BIRDS

During the Mesozoic Era, small, meat-eating dinosaurs evolved into birds. **All birds are DINOSAURS.**
#0949

Birds have evolved from **avian dinosaurs.**
#0950

All birds have a **beak, wings,** and **feathers,** and most can **fly.** This was true during the Mesozoic, and it's still true for birds today.
#0951

Not **all** dinosaurs were birds. Huge *BRACHIOSAURUS* and fierce *TYRANNOSAURUS REX* were **not** birds; they didn't even have wings! These are nonavian or nonbird dinosaurs.
#0952

There was an **incredible** variety of birds in the Cretaceous: birds with **SHORT** tails and **LONG** tails, birds with **MANY** teeth and those with **NO** teeth.
#0953

Some nonbird dinosaurs had **FEATHERS** and even **WINGS,** but parts of their skeletons show they were not quite true birds. #0954

Powered flight has evolved in at least **FOUR** groups of animals: **INSECTS** then **PTEROSAURS** then **BIRDS** then **BATS.**

#0955

Only 11 or 12 **ARCHAEOPTERYX** specimens have been found and one was a single feather!

#0956

Avian dinosaurs had **large eyes** to help them **HUNT** and **SURVIVE.**

#0957

CONFUCIUSORNIS was an avian dinosaur, a bird, whose fossils were found in China.

#0958

CONFUCIUSORNIS lived 125 million years ago!

#0959

CONFUCIUSORNIS was found in volcanic ash and silt in an ancient lake.

#0960

The nonavian dinosaurs died out in the mass extinction 66 million years ago. Avian dinosaurs survived and gradually **evolved** into the birds we know today.

#0961

209

7 FACTS ABOUT TODAY'S DINOSAURS: BIRDS!

Dinosaur fossils found in China have recently proved that today's birds are not just **similar** to dinosaurs, they **ARE** dinosaurs!

#0962

Birds' skeletons, especially their **arms, wrists,** and **hand bones,** link bird dinosaur fossils to **TODAY'S** birds.

#0963

MODERN BIRDS HAVE ADAPTED TO NEARLY EVERY HABITAT ON OUR PLANET.

#0964

MODERN BIRDS RANGE FROM TINY WRENS TO HUGE SEA EAGLES.

#0965

If you ever eat a chicken or an egg, **you are eating a dinosaur!** #0966

The smallest dinosaurs that ever lived are today's **HUMMINGBIRDS!** #0967

The **WANDERING ALBATROSS** has the largest recorded wingspan of any bird alive today. It measures up to **11.5 feet** from wing tip to wing tip.
#0968

FACTS ABOUT
8 NEW DINOSAUR DISCOVERIES

In 2014, Robert Bakker reported that a hole in a fossilized *ALLOSAURUS'* pelvis was probably caused by *STEGOSAURUS'* **tail spikes**. An abscess shows that the injury became **infected** and probably **killed** the *ALLOSAURUS.*

#0970

In 2014, a new dinosaur, *TACHIRAPTOR ADMIRABILIS,* was named.

#0971

TACHIRAPTOR ADMIRABILIS is only the second dinosaur ever found in **Venezuela** and the first meat-eating one. #0972

In 2014, two **70-million-year-old** *DEINOCHEIRUS MIRIFICUS* skeletons were pieced together from fossils found in the Gobi Desert. #0973

#0973

In 2014, a fisherman from Alberta, Canada, hooked an almost **80-million-year-old** dinosaur fossil from the water. It was set in a river boulder. #0975

Recent reports tell us that **36-feet-long** *DEINOCHEIRUS MIRIFICUS* had very long, clawed forearms, a ducklike bill, and a humped sail back—but **no teeth!** #0974

Paleontologists have called *DEINOCHEIRUS* **"wild beyond imagination"** and "a prehistoric mix of horse, ostrich, camel, and duck." #0976

213

6 FACTS ABOUT DINOSAUR FIRSTS

The first dinosaur types arrived **240 TO 230 MILLION** years ago, one of the most primitive being *EORAPTOR* from Argentina and Brazil.

#0977

The first **meat-eating** dinosaur was **HERRERASAURUS,** which lived **228** million years ago.

#0978

The first **COMPLETE** dinosaur skeleton discovered was of **HADROSAURUS** and was found by **William Parker Foulke,** in 1858.

#0979

THE **FIRST** SCIENTIST TO CLEARLY REALIZE THAT BIRDS EVOLVED FROM DINOSAURS SUCH AS *DEINONYCHUS* WAS JOHN OSTROM, IN THE 1960S. #0980

The **FIRST** dinosaur finds were described by Chinese historian **Chang Qu** as **"DRAGON BONES."** They were found in Sichuan, China, more than

2,000 years ago.

#0981

The **FIRST** dinosaur in space was hadrosaur *MAIASAURA PEEBLESORUM,* in 1985. Astronaut Loren Acton took its bone pieces and eggshell on a SpaceLab 2 mission.

#0982

FOSSIL FUN
FACTFILE

Only a **very small** percentage of dinosaurs became **FOSSILS.** #0983

More than 10 new dinosaurs are discovered each year. #0984

If you discover a dinosaur, you are allowed to

CHOOSE ITS NAME!
#0986

Scientists sometimes have just one **DINOSAUR BONE** to try to calculate a dinosaur's size. #0985

Scientists use modern **MEDICAL SCANNERS** to learn more about dinosaur fossils. #0987

In 1853, 21 scientists ate a New Year's Eve banquet **inside** a hollow, concrete *IGUANODON* at London's Crystal Palace. #0988

The fossilized bodies of duckbill dinosaurs often still had the **skin** wrapped around the **BONES.** #0989

In the nineteenth century, **American pioneers** heading west across America found fossilized bones of great dinosaurs from **LONG AGO.** #0990

Some early **American pioneers** used big fossil dinosaur bones to make **SHELTERS!** #0991

WHERE FOSSILS ARE FOUND TODAY

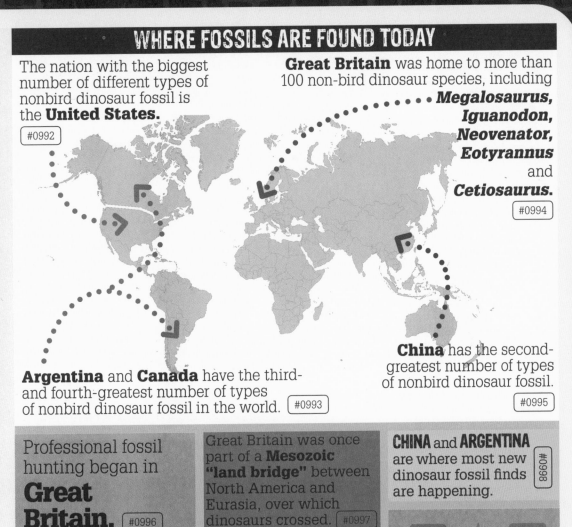

The nation with the biggest number of different types of nonbird dinosaur fossil is the **United States.**

#0992

Great Britain was home to more than 100 non-bird dinosaur species, including **Megalosaurus, Iguanodon, Neovenator, Eotyrannus** and **Cetiosaurus.**

#0994

Argentina and **Canada** have the third- and fourth-greatest number of types of nonbird dinosaur fossil in the world.

#0993

China has the second-greatest number of types of nonbird dinosaur fossil.

#0995

Professional fossil hunting began in

Great Britain.

#0996

Great Britain was once part of a **Mesozoic "land bridge"** between North America and Eurasia, over which dinosaurs crossed.

#0997

CHINA and **ARGENTINA** are where most new dinosaur fossil finds are happening.

#0998

The fossil remains of MONSTERLIKE dinosaurs and flying pterosaurs may have inspired the DRAGON LEGENDS.

#0999

A set of *SPINOSAURUS* fossils was unfortunately **destroyed** during **World War II.**

#1000

INDEX

217

Citipati 108, 157

claws 25, 36–37, 92, 94, 104, 112, 134, 139, 144, 151, 154, 160, 164, 168, 173, 180, 198, 202, 205, 213

climate 10, 12, 13, 17, 21, 59, 66, 191, 192

club tail 34, 35, 94, 98

Coahuilaceratops 57

coal mining 153, 195, 200

cockroach 23, 55

coelurosaur 105

Colbert, Edwin H. 203

Colepiocephale 205

communication 49, 116–117

Compsognathus 38, 75, 136–137, 180

Confuciusornis 209

conifer 15, 18, 21, 66, 67, 87, 96

continent 11, 12–13, 80

Cope, Edward D. 207

coprolite 54, 55

Corythosaurus 49, 205

Cretaceous 14, 15, 20–21, 22–23, 26, 42, 70, 71, 72, 73, 74, 78, 79, 87, 162, 171, 179, 184, 185, 208

Crichtonsaurus 205

cricket 26

crocodilian 9, 14, 18, 24,

25, 34, 42, 44, 69, 77, 93, 101, 151, 169, 192

Cryolophosaurus 205

D

Daspletosaurus 48, 174, 205

Deinocheirus 124, 180, 213

Deinodon 125, 174

Deinonychus 37, 50, 138–139, 215

Deltadromeus 195

desert 16, 44, 59, 60–61, 69, 86, 145, 156, 160, 168, 213

Dilong 71

Dilophosaurus 30

Dinosauria 9, 27, 194

Diplodocus 18, 95, 96, 140–141, 181

Dollo, Louis 195

Dracorex 205

Dreadnoughtus 39, 56, 135, 142–143, 201

Dromaeosaurus 144

Dromiceiomimus 124

Dryosaurus 66

Dryptosaurus 205

duck-billed dinosaurs 44, 48, 49, 62, 63, 72, 73, 114, 158, 180, 213, 216

dwarfism 80, 81, 179

E

ear 52, 53

earthquake 14, 189

Edmontonia 64

Edmontosaurus 42, 158

egg 25, 57, 73, 75, 77, 84, 93, 98, 103, 104, 108–109, 110, 111, 112, 123, 161, 173, 201, 211, 215

Ekrixinatosaurus 205

Eodromaeus 115

Eoraptor 41, 195, 205, 214

Eotyrannus 174, 217

Erlikosaurus 48

Euoplocephalus 35, 181

Eurasia 120, 217

Europe 66, 70, 136, 152, 155, 170

Eustreptospondylus 181

extinction 14, 15, 21, 26, 182, 184–185, 191, 192–193, 209

eye 34, 35, 43, 50–51, 82, 129, 144, 154, 162, 209

F

feather 32, 33, 39, 46–47, 51, 108, 119, 134, 154, 157, 164, 165, 172, 195, 206, 208, 209

ACKNOWLEDGEMENTS

t = top, b = bottom, l = left, r = right, c = centre

6–7 Computer Earth/Shutterstock.com, 8–9, 10b, 38–39, 54–55, 88–89, 90–91, 105tr, 169tr, 202c Kostyantyn Ivanyshen/Shutterstock.com, 9b, 14b, 14tr, 27br, 31b, 34, 47b, 49b, 56br, 61c, 67, 69b, 79tr, 86br, 95tr, 95b, 99tl, 112–113, 122–123, 125br, 126–127, 128, 138–139, 146–147, 157r, 162–163, 164–165, 176, 178–179, 181bl, 203b, 215tr Michael Rosskothen/Shutterstock.com, 10t, 147b, 214–215 Lefteris Papaulakis/Shutterstock.com, 11, 12t Designua/Shutterstock, 13, 205br 3Dalia/Shutterstock.com, 14tl TyBy/Shutterstock.com, 15tl alice-photo/Shutterstock.com, 15cl, 15bl, 15br, 42b, 56tr leonello calvetti/Shutterstock.com, 15tr, 16–17, 20–21, 32, 35t, 41, 41t, 57r, 57bl, 58–59, 63b, 68b, 76tl, 76tr, 205t Catmando/Shutterstock.com, 16b Kseniia Romanova/Shutterstock.com, 17t ArtHarbor/Shutterstock.com, 18cr Tribalium/Shutterstock.com, 19tr, 26bc Potapov Alexander/Shutterstock.com, 19c Incredible_movements/Shutterstock.com, 19br kaa67alex/Shutterstock.com, 20t Fricke Studio/Shutterstock.com, 20bl jannoon028/Shutterstock.com, 21tr Elena Kazanskaya/Shutterstock.com, 21cr, 37b, 57tr, 120t, 121c, 123t, 163r ylq/Shutterstock.com, 22bl, 22cr Howard Grey/Getty Images, 22t, 23l(inset), 23br(inset) Yaviki/Shutterstock.com, 22l(inset), 23br(inset) Ksanawo/Shutterstock.com, 22br sunlight77/Shutterstock.com, 22–23, 23r, 23b Ansis Klucis/Shutterstock.com, 24tl Yuriy Priymak/Stocktrek Images/Getty Images, 24bl lantapix/Shutterstock.com, 25tb 25tr, 25b, 81cr, 99tr, 124bl, 156–157, 173tr, 173br DEA PICTURE LIBRARY/Getty Images, 26–27 abeadev/Shutterstock.com, 26tcl elmm/Shutterstock.com, 26tl Fricke Studio/Shutterstock.com, 26tr alexokokok/Shutterstock.com, 26bl scubaluna/Shutterstock.com, 26br GlebStock/Shutterstock.com, 27tc Steinar/Shutterstock.com, 27l Robert Adrian Hillman/Shutterstock.com, 28–29 Sergey Krasovskiy/Getty Images, 29t, 35b, 40–40t, 41b, 44t, 64t, 91t, 104cl, 125c, 127br Leremy/Shutterstock.com, 30–31, 42c, 46–47, 71cl, 76tc, 76b, 77tl, 125tc, 136–137, 137b, 158, 164b, 166–167, 205ct, 205cb Linda Bucklin/Shutterstock.com, 30tc Fricke Studio/Shutterstock.com, 33t, 50b, 62, 117br, 119b, 149b, 150, 160–161, 172–173, 180br, 205tr Nobumichi Tamura/Stocktrek Images/Getty Images, 33m yyang/Shutterstock.com, 36–37 Sergey Krasovskiy/Getty Images, 37 Ralf Juergen Kraft/Shutterstock.com, 37tr laraslk/Shutterstock.com, 31t, 38t elmm/Shutterstock.com, 39tr Dreamframer/Shutterstock.com, 39b Fricke Studio/Shutterstock.com, 40b IsaArt/Shutterstock.com, 41c Yaviki/Shutterstock.com, 42t maglyvi/Shutterstock.com, 43t Ozja/Shutterstock.com, 43b, 204 DM7/Shutterstock.com, 44b nemlaza/Shutterstock.com, 45t Peter Bull/Getty Images, 45m Nataleana/Shutterstock.com, 45b Sofia Santos/Shutterstock.com, 47t O. Louis Mazzatenta/Getty Images, 47r KoQ Creative/Shutterstock.com, 48t Sergey Krasovskiy/Getty Images, 48b LSkywalker/Shutterstock.com, 49t Vector Icon/Shutterstock.com, 50–51 Donjiy/Shutterstock.com, 51t Valentyna Chukhlyebova/Shutterstock.com, 52–53 Ozja/Shutterstock.com, 53t Valentyna Chukhlyebova/Shutterstock.com, 53m ekler/Shutterstock.com, 53b David Herraez Calzada/Shutterstock.com, 54t Scientifica/Getty Images, 54b gst/Shutterstock.com, 55t seeyou/Shutterstock.com, 55tl, 65b, 98–99, 135, 168–169, 170, 174–175, 181tr, 190–191, 205bl Elenarts/Shutterstock.com, 56m elmm/Shutterstock.com, 57mt dkvektor/Shutterstock.com, 57l Voropaev Vasiliy/Shutterstock.com, 57m Elena Kazanskaya/Shutterstock.com, 57br guysal/Shutterstock.com, 60–61 Wuttichok Painichiwarapun/Shutterstock.com, 60tr Yuriy Priymak/Stocktrek Images/Getty Images, 60b Andreas Meyer/Shutterstock.com, 61br CatbirdHill/Shutterstock.com, 63t Frank Stober/Getty Images, 64–65 Claire McAdams/Shutterstock.com, 64b Peter Minister/Getty Images, 65t TTphoto/Shutterstock.com, 66–66tr Andreas Meyer/Shutterstock.com, 67b Cat_arch_angel/Shutterstock.com, 68–69 Leonello Calvetti/Stocktrek Images/Getty Images, 70–71 George W. Bailey/Shutterstock.com, 70bl Ihnatovich Maryia/Shutterstock.com, 71tr Michele Dessi/Stocktrek Images/Getty Images, 71cr Potapov Alexander/Shutterstock.com, 72t Rob Hainer/Shutterstock.com, 72b SCIEPRO/Getty Images, 73 Lumir Jurka Lumis/Shutterstock.com, 73tr Herschel Hoffmeyer/Shutterstock.com, 74–75 Arthur Dorety/Stocktrek Images/Getty Images, 75tr Colin Keates/Getty Images, 75cl Mark Stevenson/Stocktrek Images/Getty Images, 76–77 ideeone/Shutterstock.com, 77tr Viktorya170377/Shutterstock.com, 77b Jaroslav Moravcik/Shutterstock.com, 78–79 3dmotus/Shutterstock.com, 80–81 Space-kraft/Shutterstock.com, 82–83 Kaidash/Shutterstock.com, 82b Dorling Kindersley/Getty Images, 83tr Gabrielle Hovey/Shutterstock.com, 83c Robert Biedermann/Shutterstock.com 83b Sergey Krasovskiy/Stocktrek Images/Getty Images, 84–85 Aaron Rutten/Shutterstock.com, 85l Jun Mu/Shutterstock.com, 86tl Aron Brand/Shutterstock.com, 86tc gst/Shutterstock.com, 86tr Kayser_999/Shutterstock.com, 86br Tribalium/Shutterstock.com, 86cr fad82/Shutterstock.com, 87tl elm/Shutterstock.com, 87tr Mark Stevenson/Stocktrek Images/Getty Images, 87cl Cat_arch_angel/Shutterstock.com, 87c Martha Marks/Shutterstock.com, 87bc Hein Nouwens/Shutterstock.com, 87br Maks Narodenko/Shutterstock.com, 90b Valentyna Chukhlyebova/Shutterstock.com, 91r wanchai/Shutterstock.com, 91bl lineartestpilot/Shutterstock.com, p92–93, 93tr DM7/Shutterstock.com, 92tr Sofia Santos/Shutterstock.com, 92b Sergey Krasovskiy/Getty Images, 93tl Rodolfo Nogueira/Stocktrek Images/Getty Images, 93cr Nikiteev_Konstantin/Shutterstock.com, 94–95 Yuriy Priymak/Stocktrek Images/Getty Images, 94t Catmando/Shutterstock.com, 96–97 Sergey Krasovskiy/Getty Images, 96b Jim Channell/Getty Images, 98ct Ozja/Shutterstock.com, 98cb Ralf Juergen Kraft/Shutterstock.com, 100–101 Mark Stevenson/Stocktrek Images/Getty Images, 100tr Scientifica/Getty Images, 101tr Andreas Meyer/Shutterstock.com, 101bl yyang/Shutterstock.com, 102bl rudall30/Shutterstock.com, 103br DM7/Shutterstock.com, 104tl HitToon.Com/Shutterstock.com, 104tr Sergey Krasovskiy/Stocktrek Images/Getty Images, 104bl Stefanina Hill/Shutterstock.com, 104bc Pefkos/Shutterstock.com, 104 brt phloem/Shutterstock.com, 104brm Alemon cz/Shutterstock.com, 104brb, 105brtl Alexander Ryabintsev/Shutterstock.com, 105cl Shutterstock.com, 105cr elvil/Shutterstock.com, 105bl Getty Images, 105brl Z-art/Shutterstock.com, 105brbr Lukiyanova Natalia/frenta/Shutterstock.com, 106–107 Mohamad Haghani/Stocktrek Images/Getty Images, 108–109 Elena Duvernay/Stocktrek Images/Getty Images, 108bl Pasko Maksim/Shutterstock.com, 108c Skalapendra/Shutterstock.com, 109br Tomas Smolek/Shutterstock.com, 110–111, 130–131, 132–133, 134, 138b, 140tl, 180tr Catmando/Shutterstock.com, 111tr Ralf Juergen Kraft/Shutterstock.com, 114–115 Science Photo Library - MARK GARLICK/Getty Images, 114bl elm/Shutterstock.com, 114br Shutterstock.com, 116–117 Dave King/Getty Images, 117tr, 124tr maglyvi/Shutterstock.com, 118 Roman Garcia Mora/Stocktrek Images/Getty Images, 119t, 138t Filip Bjorkman/Shutterstock.com, 119c nemlaza/Shutterstock.com, 120–121 Walter Myers/Stocktrek Images/Getty Images, 121t Corey Ford/Stocktrek Images/Getty Images, 124tc 3drenderings/Shutterstock.com, 124br Markus Gann/Shutterstock.com, 129, 140b Leonello Calvetti/Stocktrek Images/Getty Images, 130l mr.Timmi/Shutterstock.com, 131r LEONELLO CALVETTI/Getty Images, 137c mirabile/Shutterstock.com, 141 Tupungato/Shutterstock.com, 142–143 MCT/Contributor/Getty Images, 143tr Jorg Hackemann/Shutterstock.com, 144, 177, 192–193 De Agostini Picture Library/Contributor/Getty Images, 145, 172br Herschel Hoffmeyer/Shutterstock.com, 146bl Benguhan/Shutterstock.com, 147t elm/Shutterstock.com, 148t Ricky Edwards/Shutterstock.com, 148b Rodolfo Nogueira/Stocktrek Images/Getty Images, 149t Colin Keates/Getty Images, 151 Mohamad Haghani/Stocktrek Images/Getty Images, 152–153, 179c Sergey Krasovskiy/Stocktrek Images/Getty Images, 154 Emily Willoughby/Stocktrek Images/Getty Images, 155 Peter Minister/Getty Images, 159 Mark Stevenson/Stocktrek Images/Getty Images, 160b subarashii21/Shutterstock.com, 160t ArtHeart/Shutterstock.com, 161tr Ken Lucas/Getty Images, 162b Gallinago_media/Shutterstock.com, 163tl Jared Shomo/Shutterstock.com, 166t Anton Foltin/Shutterstock.com, 170br karawan/Shutterstock.com, 171tr Ralf Juergen Kraft/Shutterstock.com, 171b David Herráez Calzada/Shutterstock.com, 179b Sergey Krasovskiy/Getty Images, 180tl Andy Crawford/Getty Images, 180c Elle Arden Images/Shutterstock.com, 181c Viktorya170377/Shutterstock.com, 182–183 Esteban De Armas/Shutterstock.com, 184–185 KARSTEN SCHNEIDER/Getty Images, 184l, 216tr weter 777/Shutterstock.com, 185tr Bipsun/Shutterstock.com, 186–187 MARK GARLICK/Getty Images, 186cl eatcute/Shutterstock.com, 188–189 solarseven/Shutterstock.com, 188cl Lukiyanova Natalia/frenta/Shutterstock.com, 189cr Jens Carsten Rosemann/Shutterstock.com, 189bl linagifts/Shutterstock.com, 190tr milo827/Shutterstock.com, 191tr Pablo Hidalgo - Fotos593/Shutterstock.com, 192bl AntiMartina/Shutterstock.com, 192t Studio Barcelona/Shutterstock.com, 194tr file404/Shutterstock.com, 194c Shutterstock.com, 194br Neil Burton/Shutterstock.com, 194bl Teguh Mujiono/Shutterstock.com, 195tl AuntSpray/Shutterstock.com, 195tr Joseph Calev/Shutterstock.com, 195c Nando Machado/Shutterstock.com, 196–197 Marcio Jose Bastos Silva/Shutterstock.com, 198 MarijaPiliponyte/Shutterstock.com, 199tr BG6English School/Getty Images, 202b kontur-vid/Shutterstock.com, 203t Bob Landry/Contributor/Getty Images, 206–207 ivan-96/Getty Images, 207t Marques/Shutterstock.com, 209tr Natursports/Shutterstock.com, 209bl Dorling Kindersley/Getty Images, 210–211 Paul Marto/EyeEm/Getty Images, 210b Gallinago_media/Shutterstock.com, 212–213 Mark Stevenson/Stocktrek Images/Getty Images, 213b Jeffrey L. Osborn/Getty Images, 214b CatbirdHill/Shutterstock.com, 215b IhorZigor/Shutterstock.com, 216c iunewind/Shutterstock.com, 216bl Andrew Chin/Shutterstock.com, 216br h3c7or/Shutterstock.com, 217t chrupka/Shutterstock.com, 217bl Coneyl Jay/Getty Images, 217br vectorOK/Shutterstock.com